COMMUNICATION STUDIES

PROGRAMMED TEXTS IN
LIBRARY AND INFORMATION SCIENCE

Communication studies/K J McGarry & T W Burrell

An introduction to the Dewey decimal classification/C D Batty

An introduction to index language construction/M J Ramsden

An introduction to UDC/J M Perreault

Learn to use books & libraries/T W Burrell

Logic & Semantics in the organisation of knowledge/K J McGarry &
   T W Burrell

COMMUNICATION STUDIES

A PROGRAMMED GUIDE

BY

K J McGARRY & T W BURRELL

CLIVE BINGLEY  LONDON

FIRST PUBLISHED 1973 BY CLIVE BINGLEY LTD
16 PEMBRIDGE ROAD LONDON W11
SET IN 10 ON 12 POINT LINOTYPE PLANTIN
AND PRINTED IN THE UK BY THE CENTRAL PRESS (ABERDEEN) LTD
COPYRIGHT © K J MCGARRY & T W BURRELL
ALL RIGHTS RESERVED
0 85157 154 9

DEDICATION
To wives and children pride of place,
To friends throughout the human race,
Lively students by the score,
Publishers, and many more . . .

Thank you all for your patience, feedback—and occasional silences—the essentials of good and fruitful communication!

Of course, on every page, for *'he'*
Read liberated ' *he and she* '
We've not th'intention to discount
Nine-tenths of all communication's fount!

IMPORTANT—READ THIS FIRST!

INTRODUCTION

TO TEACHERS, STUDENTS, AND OTHER INTERESTED READERS—IS THIS
PROGRAM FOR YOU?

Target population for which the text is designed

a) Any person who lives and/or works in a social situation which entails contact with other people, directly by means of the spoken word and immediate behaviour patterns, or indirectly through the written word or the channels of the audio-visual media. To such persons communication is a link and a tool for informing, persuading, comforting, counselling, entertaining or stimulating others. Like all other tools, its purposes, construction and use must be clearly understood; it must be safeguarded, serviced and improved by the application of thoughtful observation to a research programme. Like other tools, it will be moulded to the ways of the craftsman who uses it—and it will reveal much of his methods and attitudes.

b) Any teacher who must teach, and any student who wishes to learn, more about this vital adhesive in the social laminate than they are likely to pick up in the course of non-structured observation and day-by-day experience. We are thinking particularly of general studies or liberal studies in the sixth forms of secondary schools, in technical colleges, colleges of education and adult education groups.

c) Since we are both lecturers in a college of librarianship we have tended to frame this text rather more specifically for librarians, in training or in service, than for any other vocational group, since we are aware that librarians and information officers hold key positions in the communications network of the community, both through the organized stocks of information which they control and exploit, and by virtue of the obvious fact that these stocks would be almost immobilized if librarians failed to communicate effectively with readers in all areas and levels of society and with each other.

It is assumed that readers of this text will have little experience in handling abstract concepts in this field and little practice in the use of programs, but that the day-to-day manifestation of these concepts and the idea of a programmed text as a closely-structured self-instructional learning medium will be either fairly familiar, or at least not intimidating.

The objectives of this program

After working through the program, the reader should be able to:

a) List and describe briefly the main elements in the communication network of society.

b) List and describe briefly the main features of human perception of communication media.

c) Define the nature of information theory, its links with knowledge and belief and its links across space and time.

d) Define the nature of communication links between individuals in pairs, in groups and in hierarchies.

e) List and describe briefly the main patterns of disturbed communication as they are understood within the limited range of modern knowledge of this subject.

f) Use a programmed text in his own time and with the minimum of supervision to explore new topics of interest within the broad outline of his own experience, with the average level of success appropriate to each such program tackled.

The nature of this program

It is mainly ' linear ', that is, moving forward in a succession of suitably proportioned steps towards the objectives outlined above but having ' wash-back ', that is revision, units and remedial sequences to correct the student's misconceptions and halt any process of ' mutation ' in the concepts already established by the program, while not retarding the student who already has a satisfactory grasp of parts of the program or who retains his knowledge satisfactorily as he progresses. ' By-pass loops ' enable such a student to move ahead more quickly without being detained in areas where his existing knowledge is adequate for the purposes of the program.

In view of the relatively mature target population and the relatively loosely-structured subject matter, the teaching units, or ' frames ', tend to be longer than in many programs, with a much higher proportion than usual of ' information ' to ' testing ', and with comparatively few requests for overt responses. In this context, variations in these basic factors are believed to produce relatively little difference in achievement and retention, while tiny ' frames ' and over-frequent testing tend to alienate the intelligent student.

The teaching of concepts may be done by the process of building a relentless pyramid of evidence, or by the patient chiselling away of everything irrelevant to the concept under consideration. In either case a program could run literally to thousands of frames. In *this* program an attempt has been made to teach a concept by means of a relatively brief introductory definition with *keywords* emphasized, followed by re-iteration and extension in slightly different contexts, with facilities for access to the original definition. This has not been carried through as remorselessly as this description of our *modus operandi* might suggest, but see, for example, the treatment of the concept of ' Redundancy in communication ' in frames 164-165, 203-205, and 209.

How to proceed with this program
Before turning to the text you may wish to make quite sure that the program is, in fact, going to teach you something useful, which you do not already know. Further, assuming that you *do* learn something new and useful, you may wish to have some quantitative measure of your achievement—a ' score '. So try to complete the PRE-TEST which precedes the program. If you find it difficult don't worry, because your score will indicate to you whether or not you are likely to benefit from the program —and the lower your pre-test score the greater the benefit—we hope !

Please write your answers to the pre-test on a separate sheet of paper, not in this book, and then compare them with the model answers on the pages that follow the pre-test. Mark your answers according to the suggested marking schedule and make a note of your score so that you can later compare it with your performance in the similar POST-TEST, after having assimilated the program-content.

PRE-TEST QUESTIONS

1 How would you briefly define 'communication'? How would you distinguish between 'communication_,' and communications_'?

2 In what ways is man thought to be superior to the animals in his handling of the evidence of his essentially 'animal' senses?

3 What tricks can we play with our perceptions?

4 What is language?

5 Disregarding problems of understanding 'foreign' languages, is the 'meaning' of a word or phrase inevitably clear, precise and *universally* understood?

6 Is language anything more than a passive 'label' for concepts?

7 In a few words—of what significance was the introduction of writing to the early history of man?

8 In equally few words—of what significance was the later introduction of printing?

9 What was the *reactionary* significance of the next major development in communication technology?

10 In what ways can we communicate without words?

11 How would you briefly define the following aspects of communication: 'information'; 'entropy'; 'redundancy' (you'll know this one already if you worked through the introduction!); 'noise'?

12 What is the difference between 'information' and 'knowledge'?

13 What is (or are!) 'Informatics'?

14 What are the 'rules of communication' in a civilized society?

15 What is the difference between 'communication' and 'transmission' in a confrontation between two people?

1*

16 What factors would you consider when planning to address a small group on an important topic?

17 Can you name four major problems of the would-be mass communicator?

18 What are the social needs that tend to promote communication between individuals in a group?

19 What advantages does a hierarchy have over other groups when it comes to ' communication '?

20 What part do ' rôle expectations ' play in communication within a group?

21 Can you quickly sketch *three* basic types of communication ' net '?

22 What are the essential characteristics of an effectively-communicated message, *as opposed to the elements of a ' net '*?

23 How would you briefly define ' indoctrination '?

24 List *seven* barriers to communication between persons.

25 What is a ' symbiotic team ' in communication terms?

ANSWERS TO PRE-TEST

We can only suggest 'likely' answers to questions such as these for there are many possible answers that are, perhaps, only slightly 'less right' than ours. However, you should be able to find in your answers concepts similar to those in italics below. Give yourself *one* mark for each comparable concept which you have listed on your sheet.

1 *Imparting, conveying, exchange of knowledge, ideas, etc*
 Transfer of thoughts, etc.
 Symbols of the mind and *means of conveying them*
 All the *processes* whereby *one mind may affect another.*
 Communications refers to the *technical devices* involved.
2 Man is, we believe, unique in *thinking, learning, remembering and communicating* the evidence which his senses present.
 He has created a second, symbolic, world of *language.*
3 We perceive only *signs* and build from them our own *symbolic pictures of the world. Sensory deprivation* can change behaviour. *Selective perception* leads us to miss many things in our environment. Our senses may be deceived by *mental sets.*
4 Language is a series of *signs* and *symbols* used by man for *communication.* This, however, is only one of the uses of language and language is only one vehicle of communication.
5 The language code has no intrinsic meaning but must be *decoded by the receiver* in terms of his own experience.
6 Language is a *frame of reference*: it can *mould our thoughts* by its limitations.
7 Writing permits a subsequent *critical scrutiny* of written wisdom. Thought become more *objective*; it can be *stored* and *propagated over space and time.*
8 Printing enables the activities in 7 above to be done with *greater speed* and in greater numbers of *multiple copies.*
9 The '*Electronic revolution*', by means of radio, film, television and other facilities has put us back into a *world-wide non-literate communication system*—a 'global village'—or so McLuhan would have us believe.
10 We can communicate wordlessly by means of the following devices —*art forms; action languages; eye contact; gestures; facial expressions; body appearance; posture; use of space; timing; touch.*

11 Information is a flow of *letters, sounds and statements* that helps to *reduce uncertainty* in the recipient. Entropy is a process of *disorganization or disintegration*—we prefer a state of *negative entropy!* Redundancy is *superfluous or repetitive matter in communication.* Noise is anything that *interferes with, or reduces the fidelity of, communication*: it may be *physical* or *semantic.*

12 Information is a *flow* or *process*; knowledge is a *structure,* the *organized content of a memory* filled with selected information; belief is a body of ' knowledge ' which has *no information content.*

13 Informatics is concerned with the *sociological and psychological aspects of information transfer,* especially in science and technology.

14 Rules of communication lay down *how communication shall be carried on* in a particular community; *with whom; when; with what content, nuances* and *expectations.*

15 Communication cannot exist until there has been a *response or feedback* from the *recipient.*

16 It would be desirable to *define a desired mental set;* to consider the *needs and interests of the audience;* to choose appropriate *concepts, language, examples, overall structure of argument, vocal variety, delivery, body language;* to *abide by the rules of communication;* to *eliminate noise* and to *promote helpful redundancy and feedback.*

17 Mass communicators have the problems of : having *insufficient knowledge of their audience;* working within *large organizations;* having *no feedback; not knowing what the audience will choose to take from the transmitted material.*

18 Normal needs are : *to belong to a group;* to have a degree of *freedom;* to have *security;* to have *new experiences, success* and *appreciation;* to have *stable values;* to *participate in communication processes.*

19 *It forms an effective and ready-made communication chain; rôle expectations* are not usually flouted; active communication offers a means of *analysing the work-load* of the organization.

20 Rôle expectations constitute a *suitable context* for a message and assist in its *reception* and *decoding.*

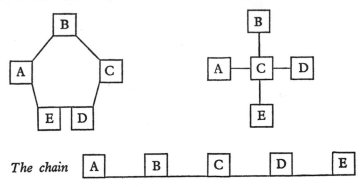

21 *Decentralized circle*   *The wheel*

The chain

22 It must proceed *quickly*, through *open channels*; it must be *appropriate, clear, well-timed, correctly distributed* to all those concerned, *adequate* but *not too long* and *consistent with other related messages*.

23 A indoctrinates B in respect of ' p ' (a debatable or controversial belief) *if B is made to believe ' p ' without understanding the reasons for ' p '.* He may subsequently be *unable to believe ' not-p '.* These results may be brought about by *specially selected responses*.

24 Barriers include *distance; climate; terrain; personal physical handicap;* differences of *language* and *social class; mental illness or deficiency.*

25 *Two persons* adopting *rôles* which may be considered to be *excessively interdependent* in a closed situation.

If you have scored more than 100 marks, you do not need this program, but—

IF YOU HAVE DECIDED TO STAY WITH US—READ ON!

HOW TO USE THIS PROGRAM

Notice that the *text* of the book, as opposed to this introduction, is divided into sections, known as *frames*, which are numbered serially. There is no reference to *page* numbers in the *text*—the *frame* is the basic unit of learning, and the great advantage of this *programmed text* is that you will be *teaching yourself* and *testing yourself* as you go along, frame by frame, usually at your own pace or, perhaps, in company with a small group.

Remember that FRAME I is at the top of the first page of the text; FRAME 2 is at the top of the second page of the text; FRAME 3 is at the top of the third page of the text, and so on. Do *not* read a complete page at a time—at the end of FRAME I, for example, ' PTO FRAME 2 ' means ' PLEASE TURN OVER THE PAGE TO FRAME 2 '.

SO—start at FRAME I; read the short text slowly and carefully; respond by answering the question marked (Q); check your answer when you PTO FRAME 2, that is, when you turn to FRAME 2 on the next page. Remember that in a study of this kind, many of the answers are not completely factual and you will have to use your own judgement in assessing to what extent your answers coincide with those suggested in the text. This is, in itself, a useful part of the learning process.

After checking your answer, do exactly as the answer-frame directs you. Usually this is a simple instruction to turn to the next frame in the sequence.

Work through the book in this way for, say, not more than an hour at a time. We don't like to mention this really, but we found it a good idea to have a dictionary handy.

If you wish to *write* anything down, or if the program requests you to make a brief *written* answer to a question, do this on a separate sheet of paper and put the frame number against each such written answer on your separate sheets. A notebook would be even more useful in this respect.

Correct your answers, if necessary, as indicated in the relevant answer frame and keep your written work, including the answers to the PRE-TEST and POST-TEST questions, as a summary of your study, until you have really absorbed all the ideas in the program.

You will find it easy to cheat! But remember that you are now *teaching yourself* and *testing yourself*—and you won't learn much, or get any credit, if you obtain high scores by cheating. (There is, however, a school of thought that admits a certain value in cheating if it makes a sufficient impact on the memory and learning mechanism!)

The program is completely under your control but you can trust the book—you're not being brainwashed—and, after all, *you have volunteered* to learn about communication.

CONTENTS

RIGHT—LET'S GO!

Consciously or unconsciously you have been studying communication all your life. From the time when, as a baby, you first became aware that the attitudes of your parents could be controlled to some extent by your cries and gestures, you shared in the joy of their response to you. So you are already something of an expert on this subject!

Why go on to study communication in a formal way? Well, we live in a vast and complex society where each individual is enmeshed in intricate networks of interlocking relationships. To survive as an effective member of society one *must* communicate and, for example, the librarian, who is a mediator between society-at-large and its inheritance of culture and information, must be an especially skilled professional communicator. Living is largely a matter of communicating, and many people other than librarians *make* a living by communicating to their fellow men—broadcasters, public relations consultants, teachers, scrap metal collectors in the street, politicians, debt-collectors . . .

1 PART I: COMMUNICATION—SOME DEFINITIONS; COMMUNICATION AND
COMMUNICATIONS

There is *no* neat comprehensive definition of communication. It can be defined in many different ways according to the standpoint of the person using the term, for it has no special field to call its own, unlike, say, geology or radio.

(Q) How many different aspects of ' communication ' can you remember in *five* minutes? List them on a sheet of paper. Then PTO FRAME 2

---

113 (Q) Can you name some non-verbal communication ploys—perhaps some that you yourself use every day?

PTO FRAME 114

---

225 There is seldom only *one* of these motives behind a person's behaviour, as we have tried to suggest in the list on the previous frame. His competing motivations are often delicately balanced in the sphere of his relations with the groups to which he belongs.

For example, his need for economic and emotional security may be taken too far, depriving him of the opportunities for new and exciting experiences in the acquisition of self-knowledge as he surrounds himself with the security which follows upon adapting his behaviour in every detail to conform to laws and regulations.

PTO FRAME 226

2 Being librarians, perhaps, we tend to think of knowledge as being structured into 'classes', and we often approach problems like this in the light of these 'classes' as defined by one of the major classification schemes for book arrangement. We chose that of Melvil Dewey and found that each main class deals with communication in a unique context and in a very special sense:

Philosophy describes the dialogue between man and man in relating experience.

Psychology describes communication as the analysis of normal or disturbed human behaviour.

PTO FRAME 3

---

114 You may (or may not!) be surprised to know that there are eight or nine different varieties in fairly common use:

1) Contact across the ages enshrined in artefacts.
2) Art forms as a means of communication.
3) Action languages.
4) Eye contact.
5) Gestures and facial expressions.
6) Body appearance and posture.
7) Use of space and time.
8) Tactile communication.

You may have noted that items 1-3 are not strictly interpersonal means of communication and that the rest are listed in increasing order of intimacy.

PTO FRAME 115

---

226 *Needs vary in strength*—a sleepy student can force himself to revise right through the night in order to pass an examination on the following day. Although we obviously cannot applaud such an approach to study in normal circumstances, at least we can see that the need for success was stronger than the need for sleep.

Conversely, we are not always able to account for, or even control, our behaviour when a pressing need is present and is *frustrated*—more particularly if we are unable to talk about it and receive advice or practical help from others.

PTO FRAME 227

3 *Religion* studies man's attempts to communicate with a reality outside himself through prayer and ritual.

Social science shows communication at work in cultural, political, legal, educational, trading and traditional groups.

Language, in the form of speech and writing, is an important medium of thought and communication and imparts structure to the process in the form of vocabulary and grammar.

Science communicates the results of research into the physical realities of the universe. Information theory and cybernetics are largely scientific studies.

PTO FRAME 4

---

115 *The language of artefacts*

For the story of pre-literate man we must rely almost entirely upon objects of stone, metal, and in certain favourable circumstances, timber, leather and fabric. The patterns of the use and evolution of such things as farm implements, boats, weapons and household goods form a means of indirect communication through the ages from usually anonymous primitive men. There have been exceptions to this anonymity—typically in the case of the rulers of Ancient Egypt and particularly in the case of the boy-king Tutankhamun.

Ekistics is the science of the growth of human settlements and with the aid of the archaeologist's specialized techniques, we may try to discover the hopes, fears, tasks, social settings and communication systems of primitive men.

PTO FRAME 116

---

227 *Motivation, perception and valuation*

Our perceptions of other people are greatly influenced by our own needs. If we admire a friend for his qualities of nobility and strength, we often fail to acknowledge his weak points—unfortunately the converse is equally true and this sometimes leads to great unhappiness.

Motivations and needs therefore affect group life very deeply and are largely dependent upon good communication within the group for their effective control and exploitation.

A newly arrived junior assistant, working in the group context of a library staff has presumably joined to satisfy certain career and social needs, on the lines of those in FRAME 224. If there is no communication he becomes resentful and apathetic—and leaves.

(Q) Can you offer an ' organic ' simile for this?

PTO FRAME 228

4 *Technology* provides the communications—telecommunications, aircraft, flashing lights, etc., and describes the part played by communication in management and advertising.

The arts facilitate the communication of emotion and emotive experience in painting, music and literature. Rhetoric and debate are the arts of persuasion.

History, archaeology and biography deal with communication from the past, while *geography and travel* describe attempts to understand and communicate with other peoples and cultures of the present day.

PTO FRAME 5

---

116 Once man begins to write (FRAMES 78-103), the task of interpreting and exploiting his graphic records is taken over by the historian and the librarian, but the concern of museum curators with objects as historical evidence continues and is paralleled by that of the special librarian in many areas for the records and appurtenances of *local* history.

It should be remembered that the 'language' of objects can be very powerful and direct—more so than words—in evoking an event, a scene or an 'atmosphere'. Note the truly expressive lines of the Norse longboat preserved in Oslo and the 'atmosphere' of HMS Victory or Cutty Sark, preserved in their appropriate environments.

PTO FRAME 117

---

228 He may be likened to a limb which operates in response to the body's perceptions and the resultant messages from the brain (FRAMES 18-38). If for some reason the messages from the brain are interrupted or cease to be generated ('noise'—FRAME 166), the limb atrophies from disuse and ceases to 'care' or function.

Motivation in industry: the division of labour

Each working group is a microcosm of the larger society to which it belongs and the history of the division of labour is the history of the way in which society developed a view of mankind based on purely *natural* differences of sex, age, strength and skill and then changed it into an artificial and minutely structured social phenomenon in industry based partly on the same natural differences.

PTO FRAME 229

5 After all that, the reference books are refreshingly brief and simple in *their* definitions:

'The imparting, conveying or exchange of knowledge, ideas etc, whether by speech, writing or signs '—*Oxford English dictionary.*

'The transfer of thoughts and messages as contrasted with the transportation of goods or persons. The basic forms of communication are by signs (sight) and by sounds (hearing)'—*Columbia encyclopedia.*

(Q) Do you think that these are adequate to convey the whole story?

PTO FRAME 6

---

117 *Art forms as communication* (see FRAME 7)

—possibly the most powerful, expressive and evocative of all non-verbal communication media. The symbols used here are more than just a code—often a comment or an interpretation. In psychological terms, they often communicate in the *affective* rather than in the *cognitive* domain; they appeal to the emotions rather than to the reason.

Nevertheless, it may be surmised that the earliest works of art had a highly practical purpose. Decorative art applied to weapons was intended to dismay the enemy and give heart to the owner and his allies. In the middle ages, the chief function of art was to teach Christian tenets to the illiterate and to beautify places of worship.

PTO FRAME 118

---

229 Since the eighteenth century a changing relationship between men and machines has developed out of this social convention and we have achieved a mass-production society. In earlier days, the shoe-maker had *made* shoes—complete shoes. Now he either sits at a factory bench making the lace holes, or in a shop repairing the few pairs of leather shoes left in use. The *price* of hand-made shoes is beyond the pocket of the vast majority of the population.

This concept of the specialized rôle applies also in the professions so that, for example, the work of selecting, ordering, organizing and exploiting books and other documents, once performed by *the* librarian, is now divided between various members of a library team. Team teaching may take away individual responsibility for the organization of learning by *the* class teacher in certain schools.

PTO FRAME 230

6 Well—the first definition did contain the word ' etc.' and that's always a danger signal!

For the sociologist, Charles Cooley, ' Society is the mechanism through which all communications exist and develop—all the symbols of the mind, together with the means of conveying them through time and space '.

PTO FRAME 7

---

118 The *dance* is an art-form in which emotions and sentiments are expressed by the movements of the human body. *Pantomime* is a theatrical convention for communication through gesture and imitative action. Art can be purely *representational*; in fact Plato stigmatized art as ' imitation of the physical world '. But it is generally held that the ' best ' art is often the communication of a *private* vision by one who can see ' into the life of things ' or who can see ' the world in a grain of sand '.

A N Whitehead has likened art to religion, as ' the vision of that which is behind, beyond and within the flux of things '.

PTO FRAME 119

---

230 American theorists and industrialists developed the idea further. Frederick Winslow Taylor, an American engineer, saw the factory as an organism and his introduction of the stop watch for time and motion studies was hailed as one of the greatest events in scientific management, and, indeed, in the whole of nineteenth century economics.

Work tasks were broken down into the smallest possible units, rigidly separating jobs which required the application of thought from those which were purely manual.

This system required complete obedience from the work force who were treated as so many units of energy in the service of efficiency, higher profits and, admittedly for some, higher wages.

PTO FRAME 231

7 Perhaps the most comprehensive definition of all is given by Warren Weaver and Claude Shannon in their classic work *The mathematical theory of communication* (1949):

'The word *communication* will be used in a very broad sense to include all the procedures whereby one mind may affect another. This involves not only written and oral speech but also music, the historical arts, the theatre, ballet, in fact all human behaviour.' See FRAME 189 also.

(Q) Have you noticed an important difference between:

a) The dictionary definitions *and*

b) Those of Cooley, Weaver and Shannon?

PTO FRAME 8

---

119 A trained intellect is not enough to achieve this vision—it needs a *creative imagination,* and the intellect may in fact be a hindrance, as in the case of William Wordsworth's grammarian:

'A primrose by a river's brim
A yellow primrose was to him
And it was nothing more '.

The artist is, however, faced with the problem of using the data of the senses to evoke a desired response.

PTO FRAME 120

---

231 This was *human engineering,* but an individual person is a highly complex bundle of needs and motives, and the newly-established study of *industrial psychology* investigated the human and social problems of the individual in the work-group.

Elton Mayo: *Human problems of an industrial civilization* (1933), who carried out much of his research at the Hawthorne plant of the Westinghouse Company in the United States, and Elliott Jacques: *Changing culture of a factory* (1951) at the Glacier Metal Company in England, both reported needs and motives other than those aimed at purely material rewards for labour.

(Q) Looking again at FRAMES 224-228, try to state what these needs and motives might have been.

PTO FRAME 232

8 The dictionary definitions are *monologic*—they emphasize the idea of *transfer*, especially transfer of information, from one ' person ' to another. This approach is influenced by the physical sciences, particularly by tele-communications theory and is exemplified in Norbert Wiener's *Human use of human beings* (1949).

The definitions offered by Cooley, Weaver and Shannon are *dialogic*—they see communication as the *sharing* of an idea or an attitude—and sharing influences the behaviour of both parties—the *communicator* and the *receiver*. This is the ' authentic encounter ' of existentialist theory.

PTO FRAME 9

---

120 T S Eliot, for example, describes the problem of the poet who has to deal with non-verbal experiences in verbal terms. In order to do this he must search for an ' *objective correlative* '— ' a set of objects, a situation, a chain of events which shall be the formula of that particular emotion ', which serves to *evoke the original experience* which was vouchsafed to him. Language must therefore be used in an *evocative, affective* manner rather than in a *descriptive* way, for this purpose.

Wordsworth again : ' I wandered lonely as a cloud That floats on high o'er vales and hills '. His poetically *felt* loneliness is objectified in the image of the floating cloud.

PTO FRAME 121

---

232 They found that many individual workers also felt strongly : —

1) The need to *belong* to a relatively small homogeneous group and to be *acknowledged* by it as unique and worthy *contributors* to the group effort.

2) The need to work in a group which offered *emotional security*.

3) The need to have *pride* in the success of the group and to share in the *appreciation* shown to the group by outsiders.

4) The need to be *kept informed* about the objectives, methods and achievements of the group.

In other words, industry discovered just in time, that man is a social creature twenty-four hours a day and not just in his off-duty hours—also that he carries his ordinary social needs to work with him.

PTO FRAME 233 FOR PART 12

9 The word ' *communication* ' stems, of course, from the Latin ' *communicare* ', meaning ' *to share* '. This forms a stem for a string of such words as ' *commune* ', ' *communion* ', ' *community* ', ' *communism* ', each of which offers the concept of sharing and participation.

In fact, Cooley's definition goes even farther than this and treats society and communication as interdependent entities with identity of interests.

Read again FRAMES 5-8.

Then PTO FRAME 10

---

121 *Action languages*
—have been used for thousands of years as substitutes for verbal expression to overcome distance or some other barrier. The type of terrain and climate conditioned the method used in many cases—tribes living in a cold and mountainous land with long hours of darkness would be more likely to use *fire* for this purpose because in the first place they would have more need of, and familiarity with the potential value of fire and in the second place would have suitable sites on which to display their fires.
—accordingly we have the Greek signal fires greeting the return of Agamemnon from Troy and the bonfires alerting England to the arrival of the Spanish Armada, not to mention the smoke signals of the North American Indians.

PTO FRAME 122

---

233 PART 12: COMMUNICATION IN HIERARCHIES
Hierarchies are characteristic of most forms of social organization since hierarchical organization tends to promote coherence and stability through a ' *chain of command* '. An important feature is the relationship of the smallest unit to the unit next above it in the hierarchy—the relationship of a part to a large ' whole ' which, in turn, is a part in relation to a yet larger ' whole '—and so on in an ascending order of complexity towards the ultimate, single, all-embracing command unit at the top of the tree.

Another important fact to be accounted for is that in a healthy hierarchy, a substantial degree of autonomy is delegated by a ' whole ', at whatever level, to its subordinate parts.

PTO FRAME 234

The term is familiar in both the singular and plural forms. It is interesting and profitable, as always, to wonder why there should be this difference and what significance it has for our study.

PTO FRAME 11

---

122 Similarly, a tribe living in an extensive, flat, jungle-covered plain in a hot land would be more likely to use *drums*—timber and animal skins would be available and the drums would need no vantage points for their use.

Sunny mountainous lands offer scope for the use of *mirrors* and these are recorded in history from the time that the Persians signalled to their fleet from Marathon, to the use of heliographs by the British army in India.

Flag signals, semaphore arms, Aldis lamps, the *sign language used by the deaf,* the *light, horn and hand signals prescribed by the Highway Code* have all been used in comparatively modern technological societies.

PTO FRAME 123

---

234 *The organic metaphor*

The individual as a biological organism may be said to constitute a nicely integrated hierarchy of, at successive 'levels', molecules, cells, tissues, organs and systems—in ascending order of complexity.

Similarly, the individual, unique in himself, may be regarded as the subordinate unit in one or more *social* hierarchies—at home, at work, in his recreational activities, in politics, in worship, and so on.

In fact, the body as an organism was a useful, but sometimes over-elaborated analogy for many since St Paul to explain the social order, the 'pecking order', and the division of labour and responsibility where specialization and independence were inversely related.

PTO FRAME 235

11 The clue lies in a frame which we have already studied. On FRAMES 2-4 we outlined the many different points of view from which communication may be regarded, on the framework of Melvil Dewey's classification for the arrangement of books.

(Q) Under which of the nine headings do we find the information we need? Look again at these Frames.

Then PTO FRAME 12

---

123 The remaining categories of non-verbal communication share the designation ' *Body language* '.

...*Eye contact* may initiate a conversation—or forestall one! A friendly glance from anyone in authority or in a counselling rôle will help the suppliant to overcome feelings of diffidence or hostility. On the other hand, we have all met the person who greets you effusively at a party while scanning the room over your shoulder for more entertaining company—or merely staring into the middle distance, probably at the clock.

Gesture and facial expression usually accompany verbal expressions and either reinforce them—or flatly contradict them!

(Q) Have you come across an example of this latter lately? Within the last minute?

PTO FRAME 124

---

235 Bearing in mind the main theme of this programmed text,

(Q) Why do you think that individuals, institutions and whole societies place so much value on hierarchical structure?

PTO FRAME 236

12 On FRAME 4, under the heading *Technology*, we see a reference to communications. Each of the other classes contains information about the sharing of a common culture, common symbols, a common field of communication by groups with common interests and responsibilities. We have here the idea of the primary processes of communication such as the formation of concepts, language, gesture, imitation and communicative behaviour derived from a cultural setting and the use of individual senses and abilities.

PTO FRAME 13

---

124 Suppose you look again at the second example under 'Eye contact' on FRAME 123—this illustrates to perfection the case of the contradictory gesture or facial expression.

Body appearance and posture can also be used as a language known as '*kinesics*'. Clothing, its choice and organization upon the person, may be construed as a clue to personal identity, taste and possibly attitudes. Interviews are traditional testing grounds for the assessment of the 'messages' thus communicated. Among Celtic peoples a shaven head was a sign of servitude and in a wider community, conversely, wigs still denote the rank and prestige of judge and barrister.

PTO FRAME 125

---

236 The answer is probably that a hierarchical distribution of activities and responsibilities results in stable and alert sub-assemblies which are suitably organized to act as closely-coupled links in a *communication chain* (FRAMES 154-156) with a very low likelihood of 'noise'—interruption (FRAME 166) from outside sources. Given effective communications, quite extraordinary feats are possible in the pursuit of group objectives; wastage and duplication of effort are reduced or obviated and coordination is improved.

Did somebody remind us that central and local government are organized in hierarchies? Ah well! there is somewhere, an optimum size for a hierarchy—they *can* grow too big and busy.

PTO FRAME 237

14 They include drums, smoke signals, bugle calls, paper, microfilm, telephone, telegraph, railway and 'bus services, slide projectors, etc.

The *mass media* of communication are simply technological devices built into the human communication system to extend its range *and* coverage simultaneously—in Marshall McLuhan's phrase—' an extension of man's nervous system.' They include the printing presses for books, newspapers, magazines and bibliographies; film; radio and television stations and channels.

PTO FRAME 15

---

126 *Tactile communication*

The baby's initial orientation to the world normally occurs through tactile explorations—feeling with the hands and mouth from first contact with his mother's breast. The blind use tactile explorations to con*tact* and evaluate the world in a similar way, also using a tactile language— Braille or Moon type—and ' seeing ' devices which chart obstacles ahead by vibratory ' tingling ' sensations.

We pat people on the back or shoulder to communicate fellowship or sympathy; we clasp hands in a handshake and the deepest human emotions have an extensive and largely instinctive tactile vocabulary.

PTO FRAME 127

---

238 In the no-doubt apocryphal stories of Latin-American armies, generals seem to be as numerous as private soldiers, with apparently equal numbers of captains, majors and colonels. The structure here is a series of *ladders*, one for each private soldier, rather than a true hierarchy.

This suggests that a true hierarchy should have an appropriate relationship between *depth* and *span* if it is to work efficiently. If a man has to organize a work force of sixty persons, he would face considerable difficulties in trying to communicate directly with each individual or even with each of thirty pairs of individuals.

PTO FRAME 239

13 On the other hand, on FRAME 4, the *Technology* paragraph speaks of communications and we recognize the *secondary* techniques which involve the physical me̅dia or 'vehicles' whereby acts or communication̅ are transmitted for all the members of the network to share—all the televi̅sion viewers on channel X; all members of the Public Library at Y; all ticket holders in the number 19 'bus. These media or vehicles (sorry!) are numerous.

(Q) Can you name *ten*?

PTO FRAME 14

---

125 *Use of space and time* brings a new dimension (sorry!) to communication. The distance which one chooses to set between oneself and the person addressed conveys a message. Latin Americans and Arabs normally stand closer in such a situation than would an Anglo-Saxon since, presumably, it is much easier to foil an attack when you are already under the potential attacker's guard! There can be misunderstandings in cross-cultural talks and the study of '*Proxemics*' seeks to mitigate such misunderstandings between delegates.

Delay in answering a communication normally suggests that the recipient rates it very low among his priorities, but in Ethiopia, for example, delay is indicative of careful consideration and the time required for a decision is *directly* proportional to its importance and the first communicator's prestige.

PTO FRAME 126

---

237 In a military hierarchy, sections, platoons, companies and battalions, or their equivalents, in other arms, stand or fall by their lines of communication which are duplicated and triplicated in a variety of media to ensure that no lives or positions are lost through lack of information in either direction. Radios, telephones, dispatch riders, are all used freely and this kind of technological assistance is vital since the hierarchy between the colonel commanding the battalion and his forward sections is very '*deep*', compared with the relatively *shallow* hierarchy between the tribal chief, bawling his orders in the tumult and the individual warriors who surround him well within earshot.

PTO FRAME 238

15 This distinction between the two terms has extensive implications for mankind which are studied in the sociology of librarianship among other disciplines. Every group possesses the *primary* facilities of language, gesture and limited mobility; only the more technologically advanced societies have developed the *secondary* techniques, particularly the mass media facilities, since they require complex and sophisticated plant for their production and deployment which only the economically rich countries can afford.

PTO FRAME 16

---

127 *The influence of non-verbal language on spoken language* is considerable. Many figures of speech have been constructed by reference to the former—' I am touched' implies strong emotion; a 'rough' or 'harsh' response to a request is tactile in origin; a situation ' smells to high Heaven ' when there is ' something rotten in the state of Denmark'; a friend is a ' sweet ' person or a ' honey ' while others are, oddly enough, ' toffee-nosed ' or ' distant ' or ' stand-offish ' (see FRAME 125 and be ready to duck!)

In poetry, we often mix our metaphors and indulge in ' *synaesthesia* ' when we speak of ' feeling blue ' or ' swallowing our emotion '.

PTO FRAME 128 FOR PART 5

---

239 The Romans, being reputedly a practical people, would have probably recommended dividing the group into six sub-groups of ten persons each, a sub-group being expected to appoint a leader or liaison-officer from its ranks. Ten is a convenient sub-group size because you can carry out a roll-call on the fingers of both hands (!) and a leader can consult speedily and quite effectively with individual members of such a small command, making sure that he is aware of all their views and that they are equally conversant with *his* views and instructions.

(Q) Would you expect a similar simple hierarchy to form an adequate structure for a modern nation state or similar-sized population? Give reasons for your answer, based on your understanding of PART 11 (ELEVEN).

PTO FRAME 240

16 Yet the techniques of mass communication—the sophisticated communications—are essential for education and training—which in turn are essential for economic development and technical sophistication—a vicious circle in which, so far, only the ubiquitous transistor radio has made more than the slightest dent.

See also FRAMES 104-108, 211-214

Then PTO FRAME 17

---

128 PART 5: COMMUNICATION—THE INVOLVEMENT OF THE LIBRARIAN
During the years since the beginning of the Industrial Revolution in the British Isles, the production and distribution of *information* has been rising on an exponential curve. Whether or not the increment of *knowledge* has been on a comparable scale is a moot point, but the *information* is there all right!

In ' The Rock ', T S Eliot asked:
' Where is the wisdom we have lost in knowledge?
Where is the knowledge we have lost in information?'
and this seems to sum up the librarian's problem.

PTO FRAME 129

---

240 PART 11 makes it clear that individuals have certain *needs* as individuals, even while they fulfil rôles within a group. They can reasonably hope for some independence of action, new experiences, success in innovation and appreciation from others, while enjoying a certain security and stable traditional values (FRAME 224). Each person should also have the right to be regarded as a unique entity in a friendly and homogeneous group and to be kept informed about the objectives, methods and achievements of the group (FRAME 232).

This suggests that even in the most monolithic totalitarian states, there can be no single central, all-embracing hierarchy.

PTO FRAME 241

17 By creating and improving the physical communications and by recording and preserving significant items of communication , technological man can virtually free the communication processes from the limitations of *space* and *time*. Herein lie the important implications of the *secondary* communication techniques for our cultural development in general and for responsible librarianship in particular.

PTO FRAME 18 FOR PART 2

---

129 The rate of growth in the production of knowledge is illustrated by Derek de Solla Price, *Little science, big science* (1963). He claims that 90 per cent of the scientists who have ever lived are living today and that by the end of his working life, a young scientist starting work today will have seen 80-90 per cent of all scientific knowledge in existence created in his own lifetime.

Of course, as knowledge grows, it inevitably grows more complex and as it grows more complex it tends to fragment so that researchers often work oblivious to related research, or even duplicated research elsewhere.

It is the function of the *librarian*, frequently re-designated Information Officer, to act as a link-man or communicator, not to evaluate information but to cope with its ever-growing bulk, fragmentation and dissemination.

PTO FRAME 130

---

214 The simple fact is that each society is a complex of many interlocking hierarchies of class (however *that* is defined), family, industry, commerce, armed forces, churches, education, recreation, cultural activities, politics, economics and many others.

Each hierarchy displays the well-articulated ' family tree ' structure of command and control with, preferably, two-way communication between the controlling individuals and/or institutions *and* the lower echelons, whose feedback from the ' sharp end ' on the battlefield or factory floor is usually a vital element in command decision-making.

(Q) Draw *your* family tree, tracing the families in the line of descent from a pair of grand-parents—here you have a typical hierarchy.

PTO FRAME 242

In order to survive we must communicate with, and receive information from, our environment. The more complex our environment—a busy college, a factory or a battlefield—the more we need to receive a constant stream of detailed information, decode it and act upon it. Even the simplest life forms depend for survival on perception—the amoeba ' discerns ' danger and takes precautions; it ' discerns ' food and ingests.

PTO FRAME 19

---

130 *Communications technology* exists to solve the problems that accrue as the sheer bulk of *information* grows day-by-day. Books are bulky; thirty-thousand new titles are published in Great Britain every year; every branch of knowledge has its own range of communications media—periodicals, research reports, conference proceedings, films, sound-tapes, closed-circuit and off-air television productions on video-tape.

PTO FRAME 131

---

242 Your family tree should look something like this—allowing for the fact that we may not have got all the names right!

PTO FRAME 243

19 This may appear to be little more than a case of 'instinctive' response to a stimulus, but *man* is distinguished by his ability to make 'sense' of the world around him. He *perceives*—but also he *thinks, learns,* and *remembers* and can *communicate* his findings to his fellows through language and symbol.

The general term for this process is *cognition*.

PTO FRAME 20

---

131 There are extensive developments in *indexing* the flood of documents by the use of techniques for rapid and detailed subject analysis of their contents and for the listing of these contents by *catchwords* (keywords from the titles), *descriptors* (name-tags for subjects extracted from authority lists) and other categorizing devices.

A different approach is offered by the *citation index* which enables a searcher, knowing of one document in his field of special interest, to trace others in a snowballing progression through the reading lists and references which they contain, as far as the remotest fringes of his subject—*if* his subject is one of those covered by a citation index service.

PTO FRAME I32

---

253 Compare this with the hierarchy of a typical public library:

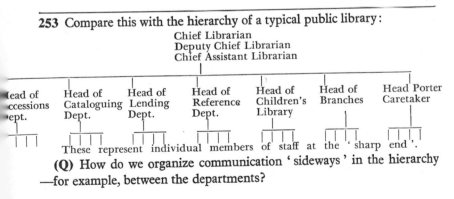

(Q) How do we organize communication 'sideways' in the hierarchy —for example, between the departments?

PTO FRAME 244

20 *Man* 'perceives', that is, receives information about his world, through an armoury of eleven or more senses. Five of them are quite familiar to us—*seeing, hearing, smelling, tasting* and *touching* for the reception and interpretation of visual, auditory, olfactory, gustatory and tactile information respectively.

Each of these *sense-modalities* provides a different type of information about the environment and normally they work in harmony to present a multi-dimensional picture of the world.

PTO FRAME 21

132 The researchers, teachers, students and others are assisted immeasurably by the aesthetically depressing but *space and labour-saving* *microforms—microfiche, microfilm, microcard,* all of which reduce the bulk of texts by a factor of at least twenty-four in normal commercial practice. In its recent development, *PCMI—photochromic micro-image,* it is possible to record 3,000 pages on a single microfiche the size of a post-card. *COM—computer output microfilm* permits the print-out of information directly from a computer store on to cassette-loaded microfilm. *Electronic video-recording* processes reproduce an hour of television programmes on a similar cassette.

All these are products of the Electronic Revolution (FRAMES 104-108).

PTO FRAME 133

244 One answer may be that since the lines of communication are normally 'up' or 'down' the hierarchy, there *may* be little or no effort to communicate 'sideways' between departments.

In fact trade union rule books often *prohibit* 'sideways' communication and direct that all communication between branches shall be conducted via the executive council or similar coordinating body at union headquarters.

At the other extreme, army units in the line find it essential to make firm contact at their respective boundaries in order to prevent enemy infiltration through unguarded gaps that are 'not *our* responsibility'.

PTO FRAME 245

21 But these five sense do not represent the whole story by any means. For instance, the sense of touch can be divided into separate areas of *pressure, pain, warmth* and *cold.*

Additional senses include that of *balance*, governed by the operation of semi-circular canals in the ears—we become seasick when these canals are over-stimulated (come to think of it—has anyone *ever* been sea-sick on an over-stimulated canal?).

PTO FRAME 22

---

133 The implications of these developments for the professions of librarianship and information science are enormous, for the *book*, ' liber ', from which we derive our corporate name (and, perhaps, our corporate image?) is no longer at the centre of our world, except in special (one is still tempted to say' favoured ') sectors.

PTO FRAME 134

---

245 The real answer is surely that in normal circumstances, all the cousins, though living in separate households (FRAME 242), would agree to meet at organized parties and joint outings.

Similarly the heads of the library departments and other similarly placed officials (for example, at a lower level in the hierarchy, the branch librarians) would normally meet at regularly organized conferences and on various executive and advisory committees.

Casual contacts would help, of course, but a family or organization that fails to regularize ' sideways ' communication is in danger of disintegrating through atrophy 'across the board ' (another pun—sorry!) (FRAMES 227-228, 240-241).

PTO FRAME 246

2*

22 The associated sense of bodily movement is called the *kinaesthetic sense*. It provides a feedback of nerve-impulses from *kinaesthetic receptors* within the muscles which keep the brain informed about activities in the muscles so that, for example, a person's coordinated walking does not require constant attention. It is this sense too, which enables you to touch the end of your nose with your eyes shut—if that's what turns you on! It is, nevertheless, typical of the other senses in its operation.

PTO FRAME 23

134 However, the problem of communication between man and man would be relatively easy if it were merely a technological problem or the transfer of an invisible entity called ' information '. But communication means something more than communications (see FRAMES 10-17). It implies the existence of people who have something significant to say to each other.

Benjamin Disraeli, when being told how man's genius for communications was rapidly conquering distances between people, remarked that the most significant and least penetrable distance was the last two inches ' between the eye, ear and brain '. Librarians must learn counselling skills and retain enough human contact with their clients to overcome this last barrier.

PTO FRAME 135 FOR PART 6

246 We all know, on the other hand, the dangers of *not* going through the ' appropriate ' (ie. largely vertical) channels of the hierarchy. Never forget the dreadful fate of the brash junior assistant who presumes to tell the cleaner how and when to clean behind the radiators—he receives a pasting from *both* the head caretaker *and* the Deputy Chief Librarian— the hierarchy has a number of these nut-cracker crunch points for the unwary!

PTO FRAME 247

23 The nervous system is an intricate system of cells called *neurons* with elongations called *fibres*. There are different pathways for different kinds of message but in normal *motor activity*, nerve impulses are sent from *receptors* in the *sense organs* along the fibres of *afferent neurons* to the *central nervous system*, either *directly* to the brain as in the case of the optic nerves, or *indirectly* via the spinal cord which, like the brain, is an important part of the central nervous system.

PTO FRAME 24

---

135 PART 6: MEANING AND INFORMATION

We have spoken at some length about 'meaning' and about 'information'. We should investigate these terms before we proceed.

When we speak of the *meaning* of a word or phrase we 'mean' that reality to which the word or phrase refers, for which it conventionally stands.

Looking back at FRAMES 59-65 we are reminded that this reality, the *referent*, usually makes the meaning clear. 'Smoke' is a sign: 'fire' is the referent: smoke *means* fire. 'Dog' is a verbal symbol: 'four-legged animal with endearing habits and a bark' is the referent: dog means . . .

(Q) Can you suggest one or two other meanings of 'meaning'?

PTO FRAME 136

---

247 RÔLES AND COMMUNICATION IN THE HIERARCHY

You may feel that we have exhausted this topic in the last few frames but there is more to consider.

Rôle is a term borrowed by the sociologists from the theory of drama and conceives of each individual as an actor who plays several parts in the course of his daily life. Any organized group is a set of interlocking and mutually dependent rôles.

(Q) Perhaps you can name *half-a-dozen* typical rôles played by most men or women at some time or other in their lives.

PTO FRAME 248

24 Messages *from* the brain travel along *efferent neurons* and are directed to the muscles which must be activated to counter the new situation as it is ' understood ', their response being monitored by the afferent neurons.

The whole constitutes a complex and wonderfully efficient information and communication system. One may compare it with the hierarchy of a library system which accepts requests for a book at a branch library counter, passes them up the line of communication to the centre for approval to purchase the book or borrow it from elsewhere and then passes the appropriate instruction down another communication link to the book acquisition unit, while the staff of the originating branch monitor the process and eventually acknowledge receipt of the book.

PTO FRAME 25

---

136 The term ' meaning ' may be used as follows:

1) As an expression of causal relationship: ' This *means* war '.

2) As an expression of logical entailment: ' This *means* that I have only 50 p left in the world '.

3) As an expression of special significance: ' This college *means* a great deal to me '.

C K Ogden and I A Richards: *The meaning of meaning* (3rd ed 1930) list sixteen such variants.

It should be clear that the problem is more easily solved when the referent is a tangible object.

PTO FRAME 137

---

248 A *man* may be the husband in a married couple; the father of a family; a motor mechanic at work; a tenor in the works choir; a painter and decorator in his recreational hours; a part-time fireman; a sidesman at church; and so on. A *woman* may be a wife and mother; a part-time teacher; an instructor in needlework or cake-icing or first-aid; an Open University student; a hostess to her friends and a local councillor.

Each rôle requires a different pattern of behaviour and for either individual to confuse the requirements of one rôle in his or her repertoire with the requirements of any other rôle would upset the *rôle-expectations* of their associates.

PTO FRAME 249

25

(Q) Devise an example of the human communication system in action, based upon an imaginary incident while driving in traffic. Write it out in not more than *100* words.

Then PTO FRAME 26

---

137 *Meaning and the dictionary*

A dictionary will define a concrete term by ' classifying it '—that is, by allocating it to its proper class or group and listing some essential characteristics which separate it from other members of the same class and related classes. For example:

The Concise Oxford English dictionary defines ' honey ' as ' a sweet, viscid, yellow fluid (class), the nectar of flowers collected by bees and other insects ' (differentiating characteristics).

(Q) Perhaps you can suggest a type of term which might offer much greater difficulties in definition.

PTO FRAME 138

---

249 A very closely related concept is that of *status*. The status of an individual is one factor in *determining* whether he plays an important and exciting rôle in society or a lowly and boring one. To some extent the converse is also true—status is ascribed to a person as a *consequence* of the rôle which he plays.

A doctor, for example, must exhibit the status of a reasonably well-to-do, well-educated, well-spoken and generally sympathetic person before he is admitted to training. During training he is popularly expected to exhibit the status of a bright but impoverished youth who works and plays with ferocious energy. After assuming the rôle of doctor he is granted enhanced status which involves adherence to a strict ethical code and the avoidance of scandal.

PTO FRAME 250

26 Your account should read, in essence, rather like this:

'You are driving through a built-up area when a child runs into the road ahead in order to retrieve a ball. Your eye flashes a signal to your brain via the afferent neurons on a direct link. The brain, in turn, flashes an efferent impulse to the eyes, diverting them to scan the road ahead, alongside and behind for other vehicles before stimulating the right foot to come down hard on the brake pedal and the hands to steer the car out of the path of the child by two further efferent impulses. A fourth such impulse causes you, after an appropriate delay to allow the car to lose speed, to depress the clutch pedal. All being well, the child is safe.'

PTO FRAME 27

---

138 Consider the following, none of which is amenable to this formal treatment:

1) *Abstract terms*—for example 'freedom' which is defined as 'Liberty, non-slavery (definition by the opposite), liberty of action, right to do, power of self-determination, independence of fate'.—*Shorter Oxford English dictionary.*

2) *The 'meaning' of a work of art*—what does a Rembrandt 'mean' to you?—what emotions and thoughts does it evoke?

3) There are '*figurative meanings*'—'honey' means 'sweet' or 'sweet-heart' when applied to a loved one.

When dealing with the intangible even dictionaries prefer to avoid *ostensive definitions* and offer definitions in almost equally intangible terms.

PTO FRAME 139

---

250 Rôles may be exchanged with dramatic disregard of the 'natural' order of things.

Suppose, for example, that the staff of Y Public Library, complete with Chief Librarian, Deputy Chief Librarian, Senior Assistant Librarian and Head Porter, go for their annual outing and 2,000 feet up in the Pennines are overcome by blizzards and dyspepsia.

They are in an unenviable plight, until little Jennie, new junior assistant and ex-nursing cadet deals with the dyspepsia with tablets from her first-aid kit and old Jack, the nightwatchman, who did Arctic survival training in the Marines during the last war but two, suggests simple routines to minimize the effects of the inclement weather.

The rest of the party, whatever their *status*, gladly submit to their ministrations.

PTO FRAME 251

27 Although we said earlier (FRAME 19) that man is apparently superior to other animals in his capacity for thinking and communicating, it must be admitted that his *senses* are relatively crude and inefficient.

(Q) Can you suggest *two or three* examples of ways in which our senses are inadequate for certain demanding tasks?

PTO FRAME 28

---

139 Abstract terms are concerned with areas of private meaning. *Connotation* is the product of past experiences, perceptions and associations and, as you might guess, this is a considerable barrier to effective communication between individuals of differing backgrounds.

I A Richards: *Practical criticism* (1929) discusses the meaning of a communication, saying that 'meaning' is a *composite*. It may be made up of a number of necessary components including sense, feeling, tone, intention, context, level, referential-connotative significance, figurative meaning, syntax and punctuation.

(Q) Can you briefly describe the function of each of these attributes in contributing to 'meaning'?

PTO FRAME 140

---

251 All commuunication now travels up and down re-organized and improvized parallel hierarchies to and from the new leaders, Jennie and Old Jack. They make all the decisions and get the party back safely.

However, on their return to the familiar surroundings of work next morning, each individual reverts immediately to his or her former *rôle* and, when memories of the dreadful afternoon have conveniently faded (or in the case of some senior colleagues, are speedily buried!) everybody's *status* also reverts to normal. Jenny and Old Jack are once again at the very bottom of the library hierarchy.

We are reminded of the resourceful butler in J M Barrie's play, *The admirable Crichton.*

(Q) What two major points have emerged from this fable?

PTO FRAME 252

28 A man cannot detect certain sequences of the wren's song although it is clear by *visual* means of perception that the bird is still singing.

The gamekeeper does not hear the special ' dog-whistle ' by which the poacher is able to control his dogs at a considerable distance.

We do not detect the ultra-violet and cosmic rays that drench our planet, without the use of specially sensitive accessories.

PTO FRAME 29

---

140 *Sense* implies that the speaker is at least saying something which, all else being equal, we can understand.

Feeling involves the attitude of the speaker towards his message and towards the receiver. For example, ' I see that Jim is about again ' gives information about a verifiable fact. It can also be said in such a way, with such a feeling, as to imply: ' Ha—getting himself into more trouble, I'll bet!'

We can distinguish here a *surface* meaning and a *latent* meaning. In fact when we ' ask ' a friend ' How are you?' it is a ' surface ' way of expressing the latent ritual of social lubrication rather than a request for information—

PTO FRAME 141

---

252 We would suggest the following:

1) Rôles and status may change dramatically according to the changing circumstances of the group.

2) The amount of information communicated to a person, and the responsibility delegated to him will depend on his actual *rôle* in the organization and the *status* which he brings to it and derives from it.

PTO FRAME 253

29 Most authorities agree that thoughts and experiences are registered and stored in the brain but we have no idea as to how this is done, nor how thorough or permanent is the trace.

The brain has over ten billion inter-connections and is highly departmentalized—but, fortunately, it is a miracle of miniaturization.

Conscious thinking takes place in the *cortex*, a grey outer area whose thickness is a measure of human intelligence when compared, for example, with the dimension of an animal cortex. *Motor activity*, as described on FRAMES 23-24, is handled in the lower sectors of the brain, especially in the *cerebellum*.

PTO FRAME 30

---

141 One cynic defined a bore as a man who, when asked how he is, insists on telling everyone at great length. Statements of this kind are not intended to elicit information but to establish what Bronislaw Malinowski, the anthropologist, calls ' *phatic communion* ' between communicator and receiver.

Tone is closely linked with feeling, reflecting the way in which the speaker relates to the audience—for example, the young man is not deterred by the young lady's words—' No *thank* you ', as long as her tone of voice is inviting.

PTO FRAME 142

---

253 ORGANIZATIONAL STRUCTURE AND RELATIONSHIPS

A *formal organization* is usually created as a tool for the achievement of a *broad plan*, often through the preliminary attainment of *more specific intermediate objectives*. For example, a public library's broad plan will comprise the provision of a service of education, information and recreation to a specific population in a given area, based on books and other media of communication.

Intermediate objectives will probably include the preliminary surveying of the area and its population, the establishment of a network of suitable service points and the clarification of ideas about a suitable variety and quantity of resources needed for the service.

PTO FRAME 254

30 Memory is still a mysterious part of our experience, with no identified seat or network, but it characterizes all animal life. When one considers again the amoeba (FRAMES 18-19) we observe that it is sensitive to an obstruction which presents a degree of danger and flows away from it; it is sensitive to food in a similar way, but ingests the food. To speak of an ' instinctive response ' in a case like this is to evade the real issue and we might postulate some capacity to store previous experience and retrieve certain elements of it as appropriate, even if this were discovered to be a function of the body chemistry.

PTO FRAME 31

---

142 *Intention.* In normal circumstances, communication is made for effect, to promote an end. Until we know the communicator's intention we cannot measure his success, that is, his ' meaning '.

As Alexander Pope put it :

' In every work regard the writer's end

Since none can compass more than they intend '.

It is quite possible, of course, to succeed in communicating an *unin*ten-tional meaning—unfortunately!

PTO FRAME 143

---

254 To fulfil its desired ends and, indeed, to achieve its intermediate objectives, the library will probably divide itself into *subsystems*, organized in parallel interlocking *hierarchies*. Lists of duties and *rôles* will be allocated to each subsystem, as we saw on FRAME 243.

As we might say of the human organism (but without pushing the analogy too far), information will come into the organization from the sense organs at its fringes (counter-assistants, liaison officers, bibliographical search assistants, drivers, hall-porters and others), concerning the perceived situation outside.

This information will normally be transmitted along appropriate lines of communication via departmental heads and the Deputy Chief Librarian, to the Chief, who is charged with making the major policy decisions in the light of his information. See again FRAMES 18-31 and then—

PTO FRAME 255

31 The units in which memories are stored and retrieved by the brain are *concepts*, the products of a *cognitive* process (FRAME 19) of thinking about the qualities, aspects and relations of objects. The process involves *comparison, generalization, abstraction* and *reasoning* and it is done through the medium of *language*.

(Q) Try to list, in words, *ten* concepts which one might derive from a brief study of two bricks.

PTO FRAME 32

---

143 *Context.* Meaning resides in the total context, not just in one attribute such as a word or intention. For example, the term ' knit ' has a number of ' meanings ' but the expression:
' Sleep, that knits up the ravell'd skein of care '
surrounds the word with a unique contextual meaning.

Conversely it is reported that when the music-hall singer, Marie Lloyd, who, by her own admission, was ' one of the ruins that Cromwell knocked about a bit ', sang *'Abide with me* ' at a most solemn occasion marking the end of the first world war, some of the ' congregation ', mistaking the context of this contribution by their favourite, began to cheer, clap and even laugh.

PTO FRAME 144

---

255 If the supply of information is disturbed or interrupted by any damage of any kind to the *communication chain* (FRAMES 154-156) ' paralysis ' sets in and no matter how alert or imaginative the chief may be, the organization begins to falter and eventually breaks down if no remedial action is taken.

It is, for example, important to have *deputies* for the heads of departments and also to have *assistants* who are each trained in several rôles, in order to maintain the service under all foreseeable circumstances—and at this point, of course, the strict analogy with the human organism tends to break down too.

PTO FRAME 256

32 What about these:
Thickness, breadth, length, colour, regularity of shape, surface texture, smell, weight, probable uses, age, raw materials, place and process of production, method of transport, proximity and alignment to each other.

Jean Piaget and others have shown that the way of thinking about the objects which we perceive changes in a qualitative sense as we grow older. Our *schemata* the well-defined sequences of physical and mental actions, mature with us.

PTO FRAME 33

---

144 *Level of meaning* may affect the interpretation of a communication. For example, Dante wished the reader of his *Divine Comedy* to be aware of three levels of meaning:

1) The literal, historically verifiable subject matter.
2) The moral meaning—a parable of man's destiny.
3) The analogical meaning—the statement of an eternal truth about the universe and the soul.

Denotative-Referential and *connotative* significances—compare the conventional, literal, denotative-referential meaning of the term 'pig' with the connotative, emotional and emotive use of the same term hurled in anger and abuse at a protest demonstration.

PTO FRAME 145

---

256 We are reminded of the story of a celebrated scholar and divine at Oxford who one day found a puncture in the front tyre of his bicycle and began to vigorously pump up the *back* tyre. A passer-by gently pointed out to him his 'mistake' and the inefficacy of this procedure, but was non-plussed by the rejoinder—'What, do they not communicate?'

In an organization suffering from interruptions in its communication chain, there is often a tendency on the part of the group leader to insist that information continue to be strenuously pumped into the system as usual, in the hope that it will continue to flow according to the normal plan.

PTO FRAME 257

33 In infancy the child normally achieves equilibrium with his environment by *accommodating* to its salient features. He *alters his behaviour* and goes round the pile of bricks that obstructs his path. Later he will *assimilate* by applying previous experience to *alter the offending element in the environment*—he lifted Dad's books off the shelves yesterday—surely he can move the bricks today!

This is said to reflect the gradual differentiation of the stimuli that surround each object in the environment and the organization of these into patterns or *schemata* which provide a basis for later learning.

PTO FRAME 34

---

145 *Figurative meanings,* rather like connotation, may be contrasted with literal denotative-referential meanings. To take a well-known text in communication studies:

'Though I speak with the tongues of men and of angels and have not charity, I am as sounding brass and a tinkling cymbal.'

St Paul is here using a figurative comparison to evoke sensory or intellectual impressions which he could not achieve as efficiently in literal terms.

PTO FRAME 146

---

257 There is, perhaps, the hope that information may be stored at the input points or elsewhere in the accessible part of the system for use at a later, more propitious time—like the captive water in a pumped-storage electricity generating plant—quite *un*like the case of the don's back tyre!

PTO FRAME 258

34 Between the ages of two years and four years, intelligence is pre-conceptual in that the child still seems to lack any means of distinguishing one particular object from the whole class or group of which it is a part. He will call most men 'Daddy' but doesn't seem to have any doubts about the identity of Mummy—perhaps he distinguishes her by her blushes as he gaily accosts a variety of 'daddies.'

Language at this stage is still *ego-centric*—a one-way inward-directed tool for regulating play and other activities. True communication, even by the dictionary definitions (FRAME 5) is not yet established.

PTO FRAME 35

---

146 *Syntax* stresses the importance to 'meaning' of the patterns of relationship between words. Over the centuries, the English language has become less dependent on the structure of individual words to signal meaning but has, conversely, become increasingly dependent on the patterns of relationship between words.

In Latin, the 'case-ending' of a noun clearly signals its function in a given sentence, regardless of where it occurs in the pattern of the sentence:

'Homo mordet canem' means only 'Man bites dog' whatever the order in which the Latin words are placed!

PTO FRAME 147

---

258 The most important basis for describing the structure of a group, then, is in terms of its *communication chain* which links subsystems and individual members of its hierarchies. We shall find, in PART 13, a strong suggestion that one of the best ways to assess an individual human being is also in terms of the quantity and quality of his communication links.

A communication chain consists, as you know, of the *possible or permissible links utilized during group activity* and it defines who communicates with whom, how, when and with what overall content and expectations (FRAME 136).

People playing *rôles* are required to communicate in accordance with the *expectations* which other people have about those rôles—expectations which it is generally desirable to foster! (See FRAME 249 also.)

PTO FRAME 259

35 Between the ages of four years and about seven years the child begins to think intuitively and learns basic physical and social skills involving estimates of length, weight, number and other spatial relationships, all based on the singularly misleading evidence (from the adult's point of view) of ' simple appearances '.

A B Two matches arranged like this will be regarded quite correctly as being of equal length.

(Q) A B What might be the child's reaction to *this* arrangement?

PTO FRAME 36

---

147 Contrast the unique message of the Latin:
' Joannus qui amicus meus carissimus est amat Mariam ' with the possible permutations of the words of the English translation:

1) John, who is my best friend, loves Mary. (the true version)
2) Mary, who is my best friend, loves John. (not necessarily true)
3) John loves Mary who is my best friend. (not necessarily true)
4) Mary John loves is my who friend best. (rubbish!)

PTO FRAME 148

---

259 Thus, a branch librarian, approached by a junior assistant who wants a day off for the races, might feel disposed to grant the request —even eager to get the lad out from under his feet for a day—but his feelings of solidarity with, and the expectations of, his fellow branch librarians and his superiors will almost inevitably lead him to say: ' No, sorry, it might set a bad example to other assistants ' (and branch librarians!)

Similarly, though possessing the most impressive facility in Cockney rhyming *slang*, or in the most heart-warming of our rich provincial dialects, he would not dream of using them on any ' official ' occasion. It would be interesting but invidious to discuss dialects which are acceptable to ' the establishment ' and those which are not. Perhaps you have some experience of this.

PTO FRAME 260

36 A five-year-old would probably be quite convinced that B is longer than A—or is it A that is longer than B?

During this period he also learns to communicate effectively but it is not until the age of about eleven years that he achieves a generalized system of concepts that is independent of objective reality and not until a further two or three years have elapsed that he acquires the ability to undertake the *formal operations* of manipulating concepts in the mind and reasoning by hypothesis.

PTO FRAME 37

---

148 *Punctuation* may be influential in conveying one meaning as opposed to another—so may the layout of the words. Compare:

REFUSE

To be placed in the bins provided.

with

REFUSE to be placed in the bins provided.

. . . we *could* reasonably object to the latter!

PTO FRAME 149

---

260 We can, in fact, analyse a position or rôle in terms of its communication function by asking:

1) How *central is this position or rôle* in the group's overall communication network? For example, is this branch librarian a *nodal point* in the network?

2) How heavy is the *load of messages* passed to or through that position? How much is the incumbent told of what goes on in the rest of the system? Is he kept in the picture—and does he contribute to it?

PTO FRAME 261

37 Jean Piaget and others show fairly conclusively that this sequence of developments is a natural pattern which manifests itself in the successive mastery of increasingly complex concepts and tasks and is largely independent of communication with adults. On the other hand, there is evidence of cultural influences on the rate of acquisition of concepts in that, for example, some societies have no interest in keeping a close watch(!) on the passage of time, whereas in other societies this consideration dominates daily life for all except the infants.

(Q) Can you think of another example that shows an overall pattern of concept formation in young children, based on their cultural environment?

PTO FRAME 38

---

149 After that brief gallop through the meaning of 'meaning' perhaps we should look more closely at—

THE THEORY OF INFORMATION

In FRAMES 18-27 we noted that any organism with sensory perception of any kind receives information from its environment. If it is able to react appropriately to this information, it will survive. When I see or smell smoke and hear crackling and feel an unusual degree of heat in the air, I am informed that something may be on fire. If I am threatened by it, I leave the scene and raise the alarm (FRAME 60).

PTO FRAME 150

---

261 Sociologists and management theorists, thinking along these lines, attempt to analyse the effect of the *communication structure* of a group upon its performance and morâle. (This should remind us of FRAMES 231-232.)

Their usual device for this type of study is a *Communication net study* which can be manipulated by strangling the communication (not the communicator!) at various points and attempting to ascertain from the model the group's probable reactions and performance in a set task.

(Q) Can you suggest one or two basic patterns of communication net which might be of use in this type of investigation and illustrate your answers diagrammatically?

PTO FRAME 262

38 There are, of course, many examples of this process but it has been shown that:

1) People who are dependent on pack animals, light canoes or human porters for the transport of their freight tend to acquire early familiarity with the relationship between the size, weight and shape of burdens and:

2) Children who have grown up in a society which has long traditions in the public performance of music, plays, verse-speaking and similar activities, generally become assured, if not necessarily talented, performers at an early age.

PTO FRAME 39 FOR PART 3

150 When we talk about *information* in terms of the storage and retrieval of information by librarians, we use the term in a more restricted sense. Of course, *this* information must be perceived, but it must originate from a human intellect, as distinct from the natural, material environment, and must be transmitted through some medium, such as a book or telegram.

Some writers prefer the term ' *message* ' to denote the unit transmitted and reserve the term ' *information* ' for the content of the unit.

PTO FRAME 151

262 Three basic patterns of *communication net* are:

1) The *decentralized circle* in which no member is central

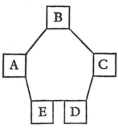

PTO FRAME 263

39 PART 3 : THE SOCIAL CONTEXT OF PERCEPTION

We tend to think of the perceiving human as a passive ' camera ' and to be impatient of speculation about the nature of the things which we perceive—after all, we *see* them there, don't we?—they *are* solid, substantial and real, aren't they?

But there are other ways of looking at and comprehending reality.

(Q) Can you briefly describe *three* which correspond broadly to the *three* great areas into which human knowledge is commonly divided?

PTO FRAME 40

151

(Q) Try to elucidate the distinction between ' *information* ' and ' *knowledge* ' and relate it to the concept described in FRAME 143—perhaps by means of a homely example.

PTO FRAME 152

263

2) *The wheel*—a centralized network in which C is central and the remainder are peripheral

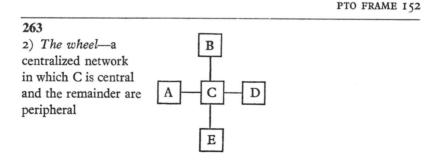

PTO FRAME 264

40 The *scientist,* particularly the physicist, bases his perception of the world on underlying patterns of particles, atoms and waves.

The *artist* has another view based on the concepts of shape, colour and texture, as well as emotion.

The *social scientist* may use descriptive analogies from either or both of the other areas of knowledge, but his world is a world of personalities, groups and abstract concepts such as loyalty, greed and revolution.

PTO FRAME 41

---

152 Information probably has less 'structure' than knowledge. It may consist only of *isolated and unrelated facts.*

Knowledge is thought of as the *organized contents of a human memory or longer-term record,* available for retrieval as and when required.

In general, information can only become knowledge, part of the individual or corporate human memory, when it can be readily perceived, comprehended and associated with or incorporated into an existing structure of understanding or *context.*

PTO FRAME 153

264

3) *The line*—an *informally* centralized network in which C is, perhaps, quite unofficially, the centre, B and D are intermediates and only A and E are true peripherals.

The chain

PTO FRAME 265

41 The point is that we do not see and recognize things *as they are*—we perceive *signs,* or *sense-data* and from these we build up our *individual* mental pictures, or even *fantasies,* of the world.

The infant when born is possibly 'conscious' only of what William James called a 'blooming buzzing confusion' or, in the words of M D Vernon, 'a random set of lights, noises, touches, tastes, without any connections or known cause,' although recent research has suggested otherwise.

PTO FRAME 42

---

153 The information that a train will leave Euston at 07.15 hours every weekday until further notice, come rain or shine, come hell or high water, will remain *merely* information to me, until I have occasion to travel to Manchester—until a particular context arises into which this piece of information can be incorporated as a vital link in the structure of knowledge about the sequence and timing of my itinerary for that day.

PTO FRAME 154

---

265 Most of these studies are carried out with four- or five-station networks. Sometimes only certain pairs are permitted to communicate with each other; the method of communication may be restricted to written memoranda or two-minute telephone calls. At others, it may be required that all communication be routed through an intermediary (perhaps C in diagrams 2 and 3 on the previous frames).

Two general conclusions seem to emerge from these studies—one covering simple problems, one covering complex problems.

PTO FRAME 266

42 Similarly, a man blind from birth, who suddenly has his sight restored by an operation or a fortuitous ' accident ' might be expected to rejoice in a world which has been hidden from him all his life. In fact, after regaining his sight, he may well undergo a period of great stress, seeing nothing but a whirling patchwork of meaningless shapes and colours.

Like the new-born child, he has to *learn* to see.

PTO FRAME 43

154 *Information theory* is a much more abstruse matter than the foregoing frames might suggest. It is a mathematical study, largely concerned with the sequence of events in a *system*.

A system, in this sense, is part of an *information chain*. A system may be a microphone, a telephone wire, a radio transmitter, a large library, the human eye or ear.

An information chain is a set of these systems, *coupled together* so that one system determines the state of receptivity of the next system in the chain, permitting information to flow into it.

PTO FRAME 155

266 1) For *simple problems*, centralized nets, such as the wheel and line, produce faster and more effective solutions. At the centre, C generally feels some satisfaction—the others become irritated as time goes on.

2) For *more complex problems*, performance differences between various nets tend to diminish, but performance is more affected by patterns of friendship or ' distance ' between members of a given net.

PTO FRAME 267

43 Another important area of relatively recent study is that of *sensory deprivation* as it affects human behaviour. We cannot perceive effectively and reliably until we have evolved working concepts—we cannot evolve concepts without constantly perceiving objects and happenings in our environment. Sensory deprivation can produce marked behaviour changes and, in fact, impairment of the ability to solve complex problems and an increase in suggestibility are apparent after only one or two days.

Further deprivation enhances anxiety and the suspicion of the paramoid component, leading to emotional disturbance and hallucinations. It seems that the brain's need for constant sensory information is even more urgent than the body's hunger for food.

PTO FRAME 44

155

(Q) Try to describe *briefly*:
   1) A simple information chain.
   2) A simple example of a *break* in an information chain.

PTO FRAME 156

267 From these findings it may, perhaps, be inferred for our purposes that the critical variable is usually the inter-personal relationships on the net—we do not communicate easily or effectively with people we do not particularly like.

PTO FRAME 268

44 Another socially significant factor in perception is the concept of *selective perception*. It is believed that we do not perceive more than a fraction of the sights, sounds, smells and other stimuli that constantly beset us.

If we are hungry when we arrive home at the end of the day, we will be looking for a meal on the table, completely oblivious to the fact that the room has been cleaned, or even re-decorated, in our absence.

PTO FRAME 45

---

156 1) Brain-human voice-telephone mouthpiece-diaphragm-switch-line-exchange-line-switch-diaphragm-telephone earpiece-human ear-brain. Unless the sound that comes out of the earpiece is a recognizable reproduction of the sound that goes into the mouthpiece at the other end, there will be no communication. Similarly, if the concept in the speaker's mind is not reproduced or matched in the listener's mind, there will be no communication. We may say therefore that:

2) If either switch in the telephone circuit is turned off; if the line is broken, or if the listener's attention wanders as an impatient lorry driver hammers on the door of the kiosk, information will cease to flow.

PTO FRAME 157

---

268 In the case of our imaginary public library, certain essential information must flow to support the structure and basic functions of the organization.

It must flow through the net in three directions—up, down and across the hierarchies. These reciprocal processes facilitate the teamwork of the organization and their paths can be traced in both dimensions on the diagram of FRAME 243.

PTO FRAME 269

45 This phenomenon of selective perception has considerable influence on the process of information retrieval from a library or information store. A vague and unqualified request for information on ' trees ' may be made by a landscape gardener who is completely oblivious to the librarian's trained awareness of a variety of interests centering on ' trees ' —those of the botanist, lumber jack, lorry driver, crane driver, carpenter, cabinet maker, paper and card manufacturer, boat builder, scout and perhaps even the dog! These aspects are *distributed relatives* and this is a case of the selective perception or awareness of one man engrossed in his work with trees.

PTO FRAME 46

---

157 Information is defined and measured in terms of its *ability to reduce uncertainty at the receiving end.* Claude Shannon devised a measure of the flow of information in terms of *letters, phonemes* (functional speech sounds) and *morphemes* (factual statements).

Naturally, the longer the chain, the greater the probability of disorganization of the message. The message passed back down the lines of tired shivering infantrymen in the trenches of nearly every war since the Fall of Jericho, started out as :
' Going to advance—sent reinforcements ' and finished in an astounded brigade-commander's dug-out as : ' Going to a dance, send three and fourpence '—*if* we are to believe these apocryphal stories of our pre-decimalization military history.

PTO FRAME 158

---

269 1) *Upward flow* comprises, in the main, reports dealing with performance statistics; staff problems; feedback concerning innovative procedures; opinions; suggestions; complaints. These are normally produced in the form of written reports and memoranda; face-to-face contacts, either casual or at formal staff meetings; and person-to-person interviews —a special form of face-to-face contact.

2) *Downward flow* is usually dominated by orders concerned with policies and procedures. Policies are concerned with the guiding principles that furnish an underlying and continuing basis for specific activities, rather as the theme provides, guidance to the orchestral or choral arrangers of the ' variations '.

Procedures represent the detailed and specific steps to be taken for the carrying out of given policies.

PTO FRAME 270

46 Much depends in communication on how people perceive each other. Patterns emerge which we call *mental sets*. We have a mental set of a distinguished professor—we choose an ' appropriate ' form of greeting and conversation when we communicate with him. He may persist in saying the most inane things but we equally persist in trying to find some hidden wisdom in his talk—we are trying to make him conform to our mental set of a ' distinguished professor '.

Another term for the phenomenon of the mental set is ' *stereotype* '.

PTO FRAME 47

---

158 On the previous frame we spoke of the fact that useful information reduces *uncertainty* at the receiving end. This suggests a link with *probability theory*.

If I predict that the next key to be depressed at random on a typewriter keyboard will *not* be ' f ', I am giving you very little in the way of useful information, since any one of the remaining forty-one keys might be struck next.

If I try to predict that ' heads ' will *not* come up at the next toss of a coin, there is only one other possibility and you would be well-advised to stop betting on the typewriter and place your bets on the spin of the coin. *More* information has been transmitted about the coin than about the typewriter.

PTO FRAME 159

---

270 3) *Flow across the hierarchies*—' horizontal ' interchanges include the discussion of problems and the interpretation of policies at regular, formal meetings of heads of departments at one extreme and, at the other extreme, casual chatter in the junior assistants' cloakroom.

This latter is one element in the informal channel of information and communication that seems to be a feature of every organization—the ' grape-vine ', which circulates rumours about appointments, changes in procedures, staff social and family events on an arbitrary route between acquaintances often regardless of their respective status or rôles in the hierarchy. This is the converse of the last statement on FRAME 267!

PTO FRAME 271

47 Conversely, if we meet a ragged old man tramping along the road in the rain with his dog we make certain assumptions—we recall a certain mental set and engage him in conversation. If we suddenly discover that he is a 'distinguished professor' enjoying a day away from the cares of his post, we immediately dismiss our first mental set and summon up the other mental set appropriate to the stereotype of 'distinguished professor'.

PTO FRAME 48

---

159 When a transmitted signal or message reduces the number of probable outcomes (the uncertainty) at the receiving end by half we say that *one binary digit* of information has been transferred—as in the case of the predictive message about the coin.

The term 'binary digit' is conventionally shortened to '*bit*'.

(Q) Try to write down a formal definition of the 'bit'.

PTO FRAME 160

---

271 YARDSTICKS OF EFFECTIVE COMMUNICATION

The 'grape-vine' has the one big flaw that rumour is always allied to anxiety and uncertainty. It reflects adversely on the authority, decisiveness and speed of action of the formal channels of communication.

Essential criteria of communication in a hierarchy include:

1) *Open channels,* constantly alert.
2) *Speedy movement* through them.
3) Messages that are *appropriate to the purposes* of the organization.

PTO FRAME 272

48 In communicating, a common fault is *incongruity of perception*. The first question has to be: 'Is my proposed communication within the receiver's range of perception as I understand it through intimate acquaintance or, failing that, formal assessment by stereotype?'

A simple case arises at the library counter when the new assistant, told to 'shelve that trolley of returned books', promptly disperses round the shelves the contents of the *other* trolley—perhaps damaged books put aside for repair. The person giving the order failed to ensure that the books to be shelved lay within a range of perception common to both participants in the incident.

PTO FRAME 49

160 A 'bit' is the choice between two equally probable outcomes labelled o and 1. When a single 'bit' of information is acquired, the number of equally probable outcomes has been reduced by half.

Thus the same amount of information (a 'bit') is obtained by tossing a coin as by discovering that a given number, x, between one and one million, is either above or below five hundred thousand.

The term 'bit' sounds deceptively positive and substantial, but it is really a negative concept, concerned with the *elimination from a situation of irrelevant possibilities*.

PTO FRAME 161

272 4) Messages that are *clear* to all potential recipients and *free of all unnecessary jargon and 'officialese'*. A message that may be crystal clear to the Head of Department who drafts it may be darkly obscure to the junior assistant for whom it is intended. Most organizations tend to accumulate jargon and Sir Ernest Gowers: *Complete plain words* (1957) gives many examples of this from a world in which people are apparently busily engaged in 'maximizing', 'optimizing' or 'effectuating'—but where the passive construction is the rule—nobody *does* anything, things just *happen*.

PTO FRAME 273

49 A classic example of this phenomenon is related in most histories of the Crimean War—for example, in Cecil Woodham-Smith's book, *The reason why* (1953). Lord Raglan, the commander-in-chief, saw Russian guns being withdrawn from a redoubt. He despatched a messenger to Lord Cardigan's Light Brigade ordering an attack. Cardigan's perception of the situation was not that of Raglan—he was on another hill-top with a different field of view—what he saw was hidden from Raglan and the upshot was a massacre.

PTO FRAME 50

---

161 There are three basic terms in the jargon of information science theory: Entropy, Redundancy, Noise.

Entropy is a term borrowed from mathematics and physics. According to Sir Arthur Eddington, it is a fundamental law of nature that phenomena must proceed from a highly organized state to a relatively *disorganized* state of disintegration as energy is degraded and dissipated. It is denoted conventionally by the letter H.

Negative entropy, therefore, may be described as the power to re-build organized phenomena from chaos and uncertainty.

PTO FRAME 162

---

273 We should list also:

5) Messages that are *timed appropriately*—it's no good putting up a marvellous book display about a celebrity on the day *after* he leaves town.

6) Messages that are *distributed appropriately* to all necessary or desirable (!) recipients, with copies to all who, although not directly involved, should nevertheless know about the matter.

7) Messages that are *adequate*, but not a word too long.

8) Messages that are *consistent* and do not contradict accepted policy or previous communications without a clear warning to this effect.

9) A major criterion is that the sender should take the trouble to ensure that the message has been *received and understood* as he intended.

PTO FRAME 274

50 John perceives his own need to borrow money: he also knows from experience that Bob is the kind of lad who would have five pounds available and be willing to lend it. This apparently simple connection between perception, experience and concept formation, the heart of *understanding*, is an infinitely rich and subtle area of operation—almost as subtle as John's approach to Bob!

It is vital that participants in communication should share a common set of perceptions and concepts. If we are talking to a group of non-librarians about library and information services, we abandon the jargon which we should use when chatting with our colleagues.

PTO FRAME 51

---

162 As *negative entropy* begins to relate random events and impose a structure upon them, uncertainty is reduced and knowledge grows. Norbert Wiener, the ' father ' of cybernetics, regarded *information* as the chief agent of this process or condition of negative entropy.

In the words of Arthur Koestler, ' life feeds on negative entropy ' and the attempts made by man to reduce entropy and achieve negative entropy and thereby improve his environment are profitably channelled into the acquisition and communication of information.

PTO FRAME 163

---

274 *Indoctrination* is another danger to which even large and powerful groups may fall victim—or a policy which some may promote.

In *The fourth R: the ' Durham ' report* [on religious education] B G Mitchell says ' The word " *indoctrination* " has strong pejorative force and its use belongs most naturally to polemics '.

The method of indoctrination is that A indoctrinates B in respect of ' p ' (a belief which may be debatable or controversial) if A brings it about that B believes ' p ' other than by enabling B to understand the reasons for ' p '. In the extreme case the aim is for B to believe ' p ' in such a way that he is unable subsequently to believe ' not-p ' even if presented with sufficient reasons for believeing ' not-p '.

PTO FRAME 275

51 We learn to perceive through our individual experiences in society and the discovery of a background of common experience enhances the quality of communication between two participants. Older couples who are happily married may, to the outside observer, seem hardly to communicate at all—yet a single unobtrusive word or gesture may trigger off a chain of shared experiences in reminiscence that is richer than any formal extended communication.

PTO FRAME 52 FOR PART 4

---

163 We can see these forces at work in a quite simple library situation.

The reference assistant is asked for information about a local dignitary. Entropy is at a maximum, for the assistant knows only the dignitary's name. He must therefore successively ascertain when the dignitary lived; who his parents and successors were; where he lived; how he earned a living; where he was buried—until, as entropy is gradually reduced by 'bits' of related information and negative entropy is gradually restored, the answer slowly crystallizes from well-structured and well-integrated reference sources.

PTO FRAME 164

---

275 A difficulty for those who dislike the concept of indoctrination is that it is frequently and in some circumstances inevitably, unavoidable—children cannot always be expected to *understand* the reasons for 'p'; often A does not *know* the reasons for 'p' (perhaps A was indoctrinated in the first place!)—and lastly—life is just too short to teach or understand all the reasons for every 'p'!

For the pathological elements of indoctrination see FRAMES 305-308.

PTO FRAME 276 FOR PART 13

Language may be briefly defined as a series of *signs* and *symbols* used by A to transfer 'the picture in his head' across the gulf to B. Man reacts both to signs and to symbols and this ability to communicate in both modes is a major distinction between man and the animals. A hungry dog reacts to food by eating it while a hungry man might well be deterred by symbolic considerations representing, for example, religious taboos if he is Jewish and the food is pork; or social taboos if he would prefer to be found eating lobster in that particular company; or taboos of hygiene if the label shows that the quality of the food was not guaranteed beyond the previous June.

PTO FRAME 53

---

164 *Redundancy* is that state or condition in which a situation contains superfluous (redundant) and therefore, possibly, confusing, matter. We eliminate redundancy (for the best possible reasons!) when we take care to eliminate superfluous words from the draft of a telegram.

Oddly enough, however, redundancy can be very effective in improving communication—especially in the case of communication through programmed texts. The repetition of keywords and phrases, the use of synonyms from the rich profusion offered by English language origins and regional usages, are essential features of the technique. They are also useful on a noisy telephone or radio link.

PTO FRAME 165

---

276 PART 13: BARRIERS TO COMMUNICATION—THE PATHOLOGY OF SOCIAL RELATIONS

Technology has effectively removed, or mitigated the severity of, the *barriers to communication* which are presented by *distance, hostile climate* and *forbidding geographical features,* by means of developments in transport and in the transmission of voice and vision by line and radio-wave.

PTO FRAME 277

53 A man will almost certainly react quite markedly to a photograph of an absent loved one, treasure it in his wallet and show it to his friends:

(Q) Would a dog react in this way to a photograph of normal snapshot or ' picture-frame ' size? Give a brief reason for your answer.

PTO FRAME 54

---

165 It helps to have certain probabilities about words normally associated together in groups when it comes to interpretation in difficult or stressful circumstances: ' Normal service will be resumed as soon as possible.': ' Passengers are requested to retain their tickets for inspection by the company's officials.' It is quite possible that, in certain situations, elements of these messages may be interrupted or obliterated and redundancy, for example, repetition, would help.

We do not necessarily criticize a message for containing redundant elements if the redundancy is useful in increasing understanding. To explain ' cataloguing ' in twenty words to a librarian is quite feasible— a non-librarian would require an explanation of at least two hundred words, probably a hundred of which would, strictly speaking, be redundant.

PTO FRAME 166

---

277 It has even begun to demolish the barriers presented by *personal physical handicaps* such as those which are endured by the deaf-mutes, the blind and those lacking limbs.

Devices and procedures recently publicized offer great opportunities, for example, in the education of the congenitally deaf; in the provision of Braille books and talking books and newspapers, as well as radar-type warning devices with tactile or other non-visual displays for the blind; and in the design of vehicles and specially adapted typewriters for the limbless.

PTO FRAME 278

54 One is tempted to suggest that the dog, having no facility for using or interpreting signs or symbols, will fail to recognize the photographic symbol of the absent person—the likeness will mean nothing as long as it remains silent and stationary on two-dimensional card, unaccompanied by the voice, actions, smell, texture and touch of the real person.

On the other hand, it must be admitted that, given some of these characteristics, say voice and movement, on film or television, some animals become quite excited at the representation of reality.

PTO FRAME 55

---

166 '*Noise*'—the final basic term in our jargon—is another useful concept borrowed from information theory and, ultimately, from science. It is used to describe anything which may interfere with the transmission or with the fidelity of the communication.

'Noise' may be *physical*, for example, buzzing or 'static' on a radio programme, a lecturer's heavy cold—it may, of course, be visual—poor register in a coloured art print or 'waves' on a television screen.

'Noise' may be *semantic*—as when a lecturer uses jargon or dialect terms outside the comprehension of his students or when a printed text has faulty punctuation (FRAMES 135-148).

PTO FRAME 167

---

278 The person who spends two days of each week on a kidney machine is able to communicate all the more effectively on the remaining five days and the coronary thrombosis victim who is picked up within ten minutes of the attack by a specially-equipped cardiac ambulance team may well survive to communicate for a long time. Social and industrial training opportunities extend the horizons of these handicapped persons and encourage them to participate and communicate again.

PTO FRAME 279

55 It appears that man's environment has a complete dimension that is unique. While dogs and other animals appear to live exclusively in the physical environment with only very limited knowledge of past and future (many dogs can apparently remember the special Sunday morning routine of the home, detect the change each Sunday and anticipate the Sunday afternoon walk), man on the other hand, has created a second, *symbolic* world of language, art, religion, myth and science.

In addition to dealing with reality at first hand, he has developed means of expressing through words, images, rituals, and scientific propositions, knowledge about people and phenomena that are beyond the immediate experience of those to whom he thus communicates.

PTO FRAME 56

---

167 *Informatics*

The theory of information includes a substantial area of study which is concerned with the sociological and psychological aspects of information transfer in the fields of science and technology.

When librarians and information officers began to study the application of computers to information transfer and, in particular, technical indexing, A L Mikhailov, director of VINITI (the USSR All-Union Institute of Scientific and Technical Information) devised the term 'informatics' for what he described as 'a new scientific discipline which studies not only the structure, properties and regularities of scientific information, but more particularly the attitudes and activities of those who produce it and those who use it'.

PTO FRAME 168

---

279 Much of this concern for the handicapped stems from one particular case—that of Helen Keller. Helen became both blind and deaf at the age of eighteen *months* before she had developed speech habits or the abstract concepts of the adult world (FRAMES 69-75). She was, in effect, completely cut off from the environment, except for the tactile, gustatory and olfactory senses, which by themselves do not add up to very much in the way of 'contact' (FRAME 20).

Through the extraordinary patience of her nurse who taught her, through the sense of touch, to parrot a small vocabulary of words and phrases, she acquired a number of meaningless sounds from which she derived little pleasure or profit until . . .

PTO FRAME 280

56 Man is not the only social animal, of course. For instance bees and ants have a complex social organization and, together with parrots, porpoises and whales, they are credited with the use of ' language '.

Karl von Frisch has shown that the ritual dance of a bee can indicate the direction, distance and nature of nectar-bearing flowers and that the other bees imitate the precise form of his dance to reinforce the message. But although this is a form of communication that is almost infallible, it is hardly a ' language ' since it cannot apparently say ' There will be no nectar until next week '—nor do they appear to discuss anything other than honey—nor is there apparently any area of private meaning for the individual bee.

PTO FRAME 57

---

168 Briefly, the new discipline covers the following areas, in common with some of the elements of communication theory:

Information user-needs and enquiries; the psychological, linguistic and conceptual problems of information storage and retrieval.

It is at present, however, limited to a few empirical laws which amount to no more than observed regularities in the use of literature, For example:

Lotke's law describes the ' propensity to proliferate '—an author who succeeds in getting one paper or book published will normally find it much easier to succeed with further publishing ventures and will be encouraged to increase his output.

PTO FRAME 169

---

280 . . . one day, when playing with water coming from the pump, her nurse ' vibrated out ' the word ' water '. Helen suddenly realized at that moment the fact that *words* had *meaning*, that they related to the environment and to each other. Her communication ' prison ' was broken and from that time her mental life became formulated and organized.

She could ' *communicate* ' and lived on to become a very wonderful example to the world of courage and perseverance.

PTO FRAME 281

57

(Q) What *three* major generalizations can we draw from these examples of bees, dogs and man regarding the relationship between 'language' and 'communication'? (Look again at FRAMES 52-56 before you try to answer.)

PTO FRAME 58

---

169 *The Zipf 'bandwagon' effect* is observed when a writer, dealing with, say, a new engineering technique, chooses periodicals x, y and z in which to publish his papers and is promptly followed in the columns of those periodicals by subsequent writers on the same subject, all clamouring to stake a claim in the new subject area.

(Q) Can you hazard a guess as to the next development in this sequence of events, related on these two frames?

PTO FRAME 170

---

281 Other communication barriers are more mundane and rather less crippling to the personality. Society is now better able to cope with the barrier which still divides people of *different* languages in all but the most desultory exchanges.

There are usually simultaneous translation facilities at international conferences. The extension of much more attractive and effective language-learning opportunities and language-teaching devices to adults and to young children of junior school age is motivated largely by the impact of closer cooperation with European countries in trade, culture and sport and by the extension of continental holiday opportunities to a large segment of the population which had formerly travelled overseas only in the tightly-knit and insulated units of the armed forces.

PTO FRAME 282

58 Perhaps these three are of most significance to our study:

1) Language and communication are not the same thing.
(Who can communicate more effectively than your dog when a walk is overdue?)

2) Communication is but one of the possible uses of language.
(Consider *self*-expression in literature and art.)

3 Language, in the sense of speech, is only one vehicle of communication.
(Consider the dance of the bees, the bark of the dog; the angle at which the cat carries his tail.)

PTO FRAME 59

---

170 It is observed that another factor soon operates to limit the flood of material, as selection and editing standards become more stringent—eventually the topic may give birth to its own periodical outlets. This is known as the ' *Bradford* ' *restraint*.

So much for our study of meaning and information. However, since this aspect of our life and work does not exist in a vacuum, it is perhaps, time to look more closely at the social and cultural context in which meaning, information and communication operate.

PTO FRAME 171 FOR PART 7

---

282 There is evidence of much weakening of the barriers to communication implicit in the concept of ' *social class* ' since the days of the upstairs-downstairs dichotomy in human relations when much of what little contact there might have been was either of a stiffly formal nature in the hierarchy of an estate, firm, household or, again, in a unit of the armed forces, *or* was, of necessity, clandestine in some way or other.

PTO FRAME 283

59 SIGNS, SYMBOLS AND SIGNALS

There is a general agreement that each of these terms is significant, but no complete agreement as to how they should be used.

Some theorists recommend the use of ' *signs* ' to indicate the complete repertoire of communication, so that, for example, language is a set of verbal signs. Tracks on the ground, arrows indicating a direction to be followed, crosses marking trees to be felled are all examples from the repertoire of non-verbal signs.

PTO FRAME 60

---

171 PART 7: COMMUNICATION, KNOWLEDGE AND BELIEF, SPACE AND TIME

Two important concepts must be briefly investigated before we look in more detail at the impact of communication on society and culture. Let us consider a pre-literate tribe whom we shall identify as the ' Librariani '. The only *praiseworthy* skills of the tribe are hunting, fishing, bone-carving (i.e. the bones of anyone who encroaches on their territory!) and cave painting. These skills have been handed down the generations from father to son. The tribal elders are the sole repository of the magic rituals which placate the gods and secure tenuous control over the hostile environment.

(Q) How can we summarize their achievements in two words?

PTO FRAME 172

---

283 Wider *educational opportunities*, especially those in *higher education*; the common suffering of men and women of all classes in *two World Wars*; the confrontation on a basis of *equality between government, employers, trade unions and academics* and the gradual *reduction of income differentials* between them; the frequent *appearance on radio and television of people of all classes* in various configurations; and the supposedly classless nature and aims of the so-called ' *youth culture* '— all these contribute to the reduction of the signficance of class barriers.

PTO FRAME 284

60 C W Morris divides all these ' signs ' into :

Signals—the physical events in the organism or its environment as, for example, smoke is a signal of fire; the waving branch of a tree may be a signal of wind; a blush is almost certainly a signal of embarrassment. and :

Symbols—things that can be substituted both for the signals and for the phenomena to which they refer. The word ' fire ' is therefore a symbol covering both the physical fire and the sign which draws attention to it—the smoke. Someone shouting the word ' fire!' will, at least for a short time produce the same reaction in people as would the *referent*, the physical fire and smoke, were they present.

PTO FRAME 61

---

172 We would suggest : ' knowing ' and ' believing '.

1) *Knowing*—the simple skills of surviving and passing time (and, incidentally, communicating—see FRAMES 115-116). The technology and material culture include only such skills as hunting, fishing, bone-carving and cave-painting.

2) *Believing*—their non-material culture embraces certain religious rituals which express their primitive ideas about the meaning of life and the possibility of life after death.

The sum-total of knowing, doing, believing and behaving is the culture of the Librariani—a primitive lot, but they seem to have the essential ingredients of a culture.

PTO FRAME 173

---

284 Paradoxically, one of the most influential *media of mass communi-cation*, the orthodox *newspaper and periodical press*, seems oblivious to, or even hostile towards, this development and one cannot avoid the conclusion that to this extent, the press stands condemned by its pursuit of profit by means of this divisive ethic in the choice of ' news ' and ' features ' and in the mode of their presentation.

PTO FRAME 285

61 The rules of *semantics* relate word/symbols to the things symbolized and control the replacement of one word/symbol by another with the same or similar meaning (a *synonym*).

The rules of *syntactics* control the other relations between word/symbols—their sequence, functions, and so on.

The rules of *pragmatics* control the relations between all symbols and their users in the social context.

---

173 The tribe has coped fairly well with its immediate problems, but, as in all primitive tribes living in hostile environments, the *long-term* problem of survival is paramount. Survival has two dimensions:

1) *Space* must be bridged in order to ensure meaningful coexistence and cooperation with other tribes in the vicinity or, at worst, armed indifference or successful hostilities. In any case, a clear message of intent must be transmitted—'Nation shall speak unto nation' and oral messages, transmitted by messengers are notoriously unreliable in these conditions, even if the messengers are physically fit, resourceful and trustworthy (FRAME 157). The social cohesion of the tribe sooner or later demands effective *internal* communication as well as these *external* links.

---

285 Even governments acknowledge that social class has lost its divisive power as a criterion for *compartmentalizing a population in the statistical sense*. They have been obliged to introduce supplementary criteria of 'economic purchasing power' and 'category of employment' which are very different from the old criterion of 'breeding' and are much less intrinsically inimical to communication except in the extreme cases of the aged and the unemployed and the impoverished who choose, or have thrust upon them, the life-style of the recluse.

(Q) List the 'barriers' recorded so far.

62 Word/symbols chained into spoken or written *language* as a form of communication, constitute a *code*. This code *has no intrinsic meaning* but must be *decoded* by the receiver. Like the embossed symbols of Braille, the holes in punched paper tape or the class number on the spine of a library book, the code is merely a means of transmission—the *meaning* lies within the experience of the decoder.

PTO FRAME 63

---

174 2) Time is an even more difficult dimension for the Librarian to overcome.

The elders of the tribe may be lost in some cataclysm before they can pass on their knowledge and beliefs. There is, in the primitive state of this tribe, no way of encoding their collective experience in a permanent, graphic form. But once they have developed a way of recording their culture, through some appropriate symbolism of their concepts and possibly of the relevant speech sounds, they are able to transcend boundaries of both space *and* time and the elders tend to enjoy a diminished security of tenure!

PTO FRAME 175

---

286 We have discussed the barriers to communication presented by:
1) Distance, climate, terrain.
2) Personal physical handicaps.
3) National languages.
4) Social class.

There remains one major area of personal and social life which presents perhaps the most intractable barriers to communication of all kinds and at all levels.

PTO FRAME 287

63

(Q) What *meaning* would the word/symbol ' dog ' convey to:
1) A shepherd in Snowdonia.
2) An Eskimo.
3) A policeman on duty
4) A sportsman shooting grouse.
5) A sportsman at the dog-track.
6) Peter (and the . . .)

PTO FRAME 64

---

175 *Communication as a process*

It is the very fact that communication *is* a process rather than a static entity that makes definition so difficult. The development of communication considerably changed man's sense of time and although we may have assumed that, throughout history, man has worked to a tight schedule with a watch permanently strapped to his wrist, it was not until the eighteenth century that even the designations BC and AD came into common use and not until the nineteenth century that we had a clear concept of the sequence of the Stone Age, Bronze Age and Iron Age. To have dated a letter 2nd January 20 AD (or more particularly, 20 BC!) would have shown an impressive degree of anticipation!

PTO FRAME 176

---

287 PATHOLOGICAL COMMUNICATION

A most vital area in which little if any progress has been made in the reduction of barriers to communication is that of *disturbed or pathological communicative behaviour.*

The mentally disordered person, whether mentally ill or mentally defective, is still, in most cases, insulated from meaningful communication with others, partly by the nature of his condition and partly by the lack of true understanding and the often fearful reluctance to enter into communication with him which is shown by those around who may all be regarded as having some kind of responsibility for his welfare.

(Q) Is this really any concern of *ours*, in this program?

PTO FRAME 288

64 Probably:

1) A collie
2) A husky
3) An alsatian
4) A Labrador retriever
5) A greyhound (or—if it loses—a pekinese!)
6) . . . a wolf.

This brings us again to perception and areas of shared experience (FRAMES 7-9, 46-51, 60, 77).

PTO FRAME 65

---

176 *Cultural differences in time scales* can be noted by glancing into any large diary—the Jewish, Moslem and Christian communities use different frames of reference for dating events as, for example, the mediaeval Christian church used the *cycle of Saints' days and the liturgical year* to measure the reality of time—in many cases, rents are still paid on Lady Day and the autumn term in many colleges and universities is referred to as the Michaelmas term.

There is a parallel here with the use of social time cycles in more primitive societies, based on the *natural cycles of the moon, the seasons, crops and herds.*

In fact, our *linear concept of time* is relatively new in the history of man and is a more truly philosophical or scientific reckoning of *progress* or ' *process* '.

PTO FRAME 177

---

288 *This* area may be considered to be the particular province of professionally-qualified and experienced people whose chosen task it is to deal with individual or social pathology. But since most of us are called upon to judge, serve and manipulate other people almost every day and communicate with them constantly in the process, making assumptions which are related to constantly changing circumstances as we do so, the more we know about the circumstances of the mentally disordered, diagnosed or not diagnosed, the more effective and mutually helpful will be our dialogue with them in professional and social relations.

PTO FRAME 289

65 The term '*icon*' is often used when the symbol is recognizably like its referent—for example, the international icons on the doors of ladies' and gentlemen's toilets; the identification of saints by the instrument of their martyrdom—St Andrew's cross, St Catherine's wheel; the road signs with human figures which warn the driver of the proximity of a school and those which control pedestrian crossings in towns.

The term *symbolism* is also used to describe the characteristic technique with which some writers invest objects and ideas with a representative significance—' La belle dame sans merci '; ' The four horsemen of the Apocalypse '; ' the red badge of courage '.

PTO FRAME 66

---

177 Five hundred years before the birth of Christ, the Greek philosopher Heraclitus, exemplified the concept of progress or ' process ' by saying: ' No man can step twice into the same river '. This view is inextricably woven into contemporary views of science which, after the time of Isaac Newton, divided the world into ' things ' (independent static entities) and ' processes '.

Early work in the design of subject headings under which to list documents in catalogues and bibliographies, indicated a similar outlook and this technique is still found to be of value.

METALS : ELECTROPLATING

LITERATURE : CRITICISM.

ie ' thing ' and ' activity ' or process.

PTO FRAME 178

---

289 It is feasible and useful to formulate a *rationale of human problems in terms of ' communication '*, along a spectrum which ranges from the ' normal ' to the ' severely abnormal ', disturbance being regarded as either a functional mutation or a form of inter-personal or inter-group exchange which appears to be inappropriate to the social situation in which it occurs—which is, in other words, ' eccentric '.

(**Q**) Does this add anything to *our* study and practice of communication?

PTO FRAME 290

66 Marshall McLuhan divides the further communications history of mankind into three major phases:

1) The *spoken* language.
2) The *written* language.
3) The *printed* language.

PTO FRAME 67

---

178 The revolution in philosophy brought about by the *theory of relativity* and by the work of Bertrand Russell and A N Whitehead, suggested, however, that a given object could only be described in terms of its relationships to other objects and in terms of the fact that each object, far from being static, is *constantly changing*.

A view of reality as a ' process ' is now firmly established along these lines and any attempt to describe a phenomenon such as communication must proceed by arresting for a moment the dynamic of the *process* of the phenomenon, rather as a ' still ' photograph is extracted from a film or a football match as a split-second of ' frozen ' activity.

PTO FRAME 179

---

290 It means that communication may be regarded as a *diagnostic indicator* of constantly fluctuating human relationships which are otherwise difficult to ' fix ' for study or repair as gestalt ' wholes ' (see FRAME 178 above).

We owe to Freud at the end of the nineteenth century and to Ruesch in recent years this recognition that the content of a message is a function of the human relationship which it serves and, as such, is the main link between members of a pair or group.

PTO FRAME 291

Before the development of the alphabet, according to McLuhan, man lived in full communion with his fellows. Social space was delineated by range of earshot and people kept to the area where all the talk went on —the Forum, the courtyard of the chief's kraal, or some similar location.

In the absence of *written* history, the accumulated lore and wisdom of the group was handed on from generation to generation by word of mouth; in the absence of *libraries* the retentive memories of elders and minstrels had to record and store the rituals, genealogies and necessary customs of the tribe.

PTO FRAME 68

---

179 But just as the ' still " photograph gives a very limited impression of the film or match (and in fact may be deliberately chosen to represent the original for just that reason!) so communication models, no matter how complex, can be misleading. There is no evidence that communication is as simple and ' linear ' a process as the film or match from which the ' still ' is taken—there is no discernible beginning and no predictable end—and models cannot be made complex enough to give any idea of the vitally important social and cultural situations in which communication pursues its cork-screw cycles.

PTO FRAME 180 FOR PART 8

---

291 It is possible to distinguish disturbances in the following communication functions:

1) Input (perception) and output (movement and speech).
2) Retention, recall and recognition.
3) Thinking, judgement, decision-making.
4) Consciousness, conflict and defence in relation to outside stimuli.
5) Physical, social and emotional growth, learning and maturation, especially in the matter of adapting to existing communication systems in the environment—systems which may themselves be imperfect or inadequate.

(Q) Can you suggest a major factor in the incidence of disturbed communication? (See FRAMES 69-75) then

PTO FRAME 292

The only possible technology available to maintain accuracy and fidelity to the originals in the act of transmission was that of the rhythmic phrase—here were the origins of poetry which became, for pre-literate man a combined archive, encyclopaedia, scripture and guide for living in the hands of the Celtic bards, the Anglo-Saxon 'scops' and the Scandinavian 'scalds'.

So much for the social importance of the spoken language in pre-literate societies. It is appropriate now to consider briefly some theories of language development in the individual.

PTO FRAME 69

---

180 PART 8: COMMUNICATION, SOCIETY AND CULTURE

There are at least two important determinants in the growth of the communication function of an individual member of human society:

1) *The biological development* of the human being is influential in the growth of communication within the human organism (FRAMES 18-38) since *genes* act as biological information centres in determining the sequence of physical maturation.

PTO FRAME 181

---

292 THE CHILD AND FEEDBACK IN COMMUNICATION

Age is a very important consideration in the study of disturbed or pathological communication. Participation in a two-way communication system with its mother or mother-substitute is essential if a child is to survive as a healthy and effective person and this participation may well begin with the mother's response to her child's first cry—the point at which, perhaps, the child first perceives that he has been acknowledged.

PTO FRAME 293

This area is a battle-ground for psycho-linguists. One school of thought, led by B F Skinner, maintains that language is learned through a '*stimulus-response*' mechanism—the knowledge that certain sounds will probably result in the satisfaction of certain needs.

The other school of thought, supported by Noam Chomsky, asserts that the child's *intuitive* knowledge of grammar must be due to the presence of deep '*structures*', like concealed railway lines, which enable the child to frame speech-language in an infinite number of variations.

PTO FRAME 70

---

181 2) A *favourable social environment* contributes to the growth of communication with other human beings by providing environmental opportunities for association and cooperation in society and by encouraging the emergence of knowledge, skills, beliefs and acceptable patterns of behaviour (see FRAMES 171-174)—in other words, a complete culture which provides the *substance* for messages and the *rules* for their effective and considerate communication. See FRAMES 186, 190, 209 if you would like to pursue this matter of ' rules ' now—but in any case eventually—

—PTO FRAME 182

---

293 In the years that follow, up to and beyond biological maturity, one of the most important conditions for development is *the opportunity to learn to participate in satisfying and effective communication systems,* but, apart from the barriers of environment and disability which have already been discussed, there are numerous situations in which such an opportunity is withheld, wholly or partially, from the child.

An infant whose early attempts to communicate are not acknowledged, or acknowledged only grudgingly and spasmodically, has no '*feedback*' (see FRAMES 194-198 and 213-214) from which to assess his progress in relating.

(Q) In what ways might feedback be inadequate?

PTO FRAME 294

70 *A baby's crying* is the beginning of his language, although in the first hours of his life he is, no doubt, merely trying to clear and exercise his lungs. Nevertheless, as soon as his cries produce a *response* in his mother, communication between the two has begun even though the baby's reactions continue for some time to be *reflexive* as he reacts to the confusion of the world and to his own bodily chemistry.

Differentiated crying indicates that, although the cry continues to be a total bodily response to situations, nevertheless after the first month of life the type of response begins to vary according to the nature of the situation. For example, hunger causes muscle contractions and produces a characteristic 'hungry cry'.

PTO FRAME 71

---

182 Although there are many definitions of '*culture*', it is usually more helpful to say what it *does* rather than to try to define what it *is*.

Culture serves as a *medium* through which human minds interact with each other in, for example, communication. Compare with this, the ideas concerning the transmission of *light* through a 'medium'. Banesh Hoffman: *Strange story of the quantum* (1963) tells how the Greeks came to believe that *something* must bridge the gap between our eyes and the objects which we see and proceeded to invest 'it' with an objective reality, study 'it' and invent theories about 'it'.

PTO FRAME 183

---

294 Feedback may be *inadequate* or *inappropriate*, or both, and if thus adopted as a general attitude by the responding parent, it will produce disappointment and disturbance in the sender of the original message:

Child: 'I'm cold and wet, Dad, may we go home?'
Parent: 'Never mind—we'll see' or:
'It's only three weeks to Christmas' *or even*:
'Arsenal have lost again'

Feedback may be deliberately *selective*, as one suspects in the last of these three responses, to a particular area of interest to the parent—in this case—football—to which it may be hoped to win the child's allegiance —even though it may not correspond with *his* interests or abilities.

PTO FRAME 295

71 *Patterned responses* emerge gradually as fixed complexes of movements and cries, each a response to a given situation. By means of these patterned responses the infant can begin to control and modify his environment to satisfy his needs—he yells and grimaces: mother reacts: discomfort disappears.

Babbling follows at about the third or fourth month as a form of vocal play, during which the child becomes responsive to sounds around him —a very important stage of development.

Lallation usually begins sometime after the age of six months—it is purposeful imitation of sounds around him which he finds pleasurable and is contrasted with—

PTO FRAME 72

---

183 John Donne perpetuated this conceit in his poem *The ecstasy*:
' Our eye-beams twisted, and did thread
Our eyes upon one double string '.
Although he tells us also that ' no man is an island ', we must differ from his judgement and claim that, just as the Greeks must have secretly doubted the objective reality of the ' eye-beams ', so each man must secretly doubt Donne's claim and remain convinced of his insularity until the medium of culture, like the culture medium used in the biological sciences, creates the conditions for development.

PTO FRAME 184

---

295 Selectivity of response may lie in the *degree of detail* offered to the child, so that he cannot learn or continue to learn from responses that are too meagre or too detailed for his needs. Alternatively, responses may be made in only one, possibly inappropriate, *mode of ' language '*— verbal language or action language, it matters little—so that in extreme cases the child may grow up to communicate largely, or even exclusively, in that form of expression which figured so largely in his childhood, for example, mindless violence.

Further than this, it is doubly effective to acknowledge the child's attempt to communicate *in the same mode in which he makes it*—for example, by sniffing at the perfume of the rose which he holds up and then going on to comment in some other mode—in words or a picture or by touch—all based on a shared inter-personal planned activity *preparatory to further communication.*

PTO FRAME 296

72 —*Echolalia,* the imitation from about the ninth or tenth month of sounds made by other *people* around him—an early phase of conscious communication. The repertoire of sounds thus built up becomes a basis for the formation of:

Words from the age of about one year. If the child is not handicapped by hearing loss or speech impediment, he will continue to form simple *two and three word sentences* by the age of two years and *by the age of four years he will have mastered the entire complex and abstract grammatical structure of his country's language.* This stunning intellectual achievement which is so often taken for granted, is performed as a routine by every normal child in all but the most soul-destroying environments.

PTO FRAME 73

---

184 Culture also provides a *frame of reference* of partially-shared understandings—it provides the basis upon which sympathy and cooperation are possible. As we said earlier (FRAME 181), it provides the rules for human interaction.

If you are to cooperate with someone else, you must be able to predict his actions and reactions—in tennis or football you must be able to rely upon his knowing and accepting the rules of the game and, in view of the fact that you have both presumably inherited this element of your common culture, you should be able to predict even his tactics.

PTO FRAME 185

---

296 Parents may similarly react, through ignorance or lack of imagination to the *literal denotative meanings of words* used by their children, and fail to respond, or respond only in a derogatory way, to the equally important subjective connotative statements, producing distortions in the child's view of life in general and of communications in particular.

' It's dark in here, Dad '—a child expressing apprehension and looking for comfort is hardly comforted by Dad's realistic ' denotative ' assessment that ' It's not completely dark, there's a little light under the door '.

PTO FRAME 297

73 There is so much that we do not know about language—we are still very unsure of the factors in a child's *linguistic development* and in the *acquisition of reading facility*—we still do not know much about the relationship between language and the *acquisition of knowledge*.

We still know very little about the *natural and artificial barriers* that may impede communication by spoken language, but for an outline of the story of Helen Keller see FRAMES 279-280.

We are still unclear about the *origins in pre-history* of the sets of largely arbitrary verbal symbols, their internal structures and overt meanings which constitute the code of *speech-communication*.

PTO FRAME 74

---

185 We always feel wary when we encounter someone from a strange culture because the symbols, and often the content, of his communication are unfamiliar and his ' tactics ' unpredictable. Although each of us is, indeed, a private self built up from our own unique experiences and reactions, we can more readily identify with the experiences of others, which, though not identical with our own, are recognizably similar in kind and context and conform to rules which are, at least, known to us and to which we may readily subscribe.

(Q) Perhaps this would be a good opportunity to take a break and list, say, *five* or *six categories of rules* by which one's cultural background might control one's communication with others.

PTO FRAME 186

---

297 A parent may also show impatience with a child's vestigial *action-based communications* and respond with completely verbalized acknowledgements which the child cannot as yet understand and which consequently tend to block new growth as surely as does insistence on the maintenance of obsolete methods of communication. It is vital to *time new departures in communication* to coincide with *strategic moments in the child's development*.

PTO FRAME 298

74 *Private use of language and its public consequences*

When a child has learned to use words he is thereby enabled to communicate with his environment without directly contacting or manipulating it. He can deal with things not actually present, with situations *not here* and *not now*.

He can *think* and simultaneously becomes conscious of the influence he can exert. Language, through *consciousness*, becomes a medium for *self-development*, for access to a *new store of social experience* at second hand, for the formation of *abstract concepts*.

PTO FRAME 75

---

186 *Rules* about communication are essential to guide individuals in such matters as:

1) *With whom* they should communicate in various situations.

2) *How* they should communicate—in what ' language '.

3) *When* they should communicate—the question of ' tact '.

4) *What content* should, or should not, be communicated in various situations.

5) *What nuances and concealed meanings* might be employed.

6) *What degree of reaction* is appropriate to a given item of communication by either party.

Custom and convention are parts of the cultural inheritance which help individuals in these matters, to guide them in the decision about whether or not to ' keep a stiff upper lip ', for example.

PTO FRAME 187

---

298 *Contradictions, inconsistencies, ambiguities and disorganization in daily life* are further offences against the overall pattern of existence which is so important a frame of reference to most children and young people. Such offences may lead to confusion and withdrawal from meaningful communication.

Overt anxiety display by an adult while seeking to comfort an apprehensive youngster is again a source of bewilderment to him and increases his alarm.

In such emergencies, emotion often binds people together when words fail, but emotion which is inconsistent with the perceived context tends to diminish such bonds and repress communication.

PTO FRAME 299

75 This *private use of language* for problem solving, for reminiscing, for ' companionship' in a solitary situation is a product of *thought*: it is, as Plato described it, ' the soul talking to itself '.

We may use private language in this way, also for rehearsing a conversation, discussion or interview which we are about to share—as G H Mead puts it: ' We take on the rôle of the (generalized) other '.

It is the medium for expressing our concept of ' *self* ' and the child chatting to himself thus in *egocentric language* is often exploring and consolidating this important concept.

(Q) Do you think that language can be even more influential than a mere system of ' labels ' for objects and activities? If so—how?

PTO FRAME 76

---

187 It is important to realize that communication is not a remote phenomenon—it is difficult, therefore, for us to examine it in a detached and objective manner since the need for communication is just as much a part of man's nature as are his biological needs.

Starve a child of food and he will die; starve him of human company and he will progress barely beyond the stage of the animal. So-called *feral children*, babies brought up in the wild with a minimum of human contact, have been found but have never been able to rejoin society in the full communicative sense.

PTO FRAME 188

---

299 Indeed, on occasion *communication may cease altogether*—the little boy at the bus-stop or in the darkened room gets no reply at all. Alternatively, the environment of the relationship is filled with *continuous, meaningless chatter* that is just as frustrating as silence and just as likely to lead to deep disturbance.

Further communication is inhibited and, in extreme cases, the *deliberate pursuit of misunderstanding and disagreement* on the part of the respondent-parent becomes of pathological dimensions with extremely distressing consequences for all concerned.

PTO FRAME 300

According to scholars like Edward Sapir and Benjamin Whorf, language is not only a system of labels for things that seem relevant to us in our planning, problem-solving, rehearsing and reminiscing. It can, in various subtle ways, *determine what we perceive, experience and think*, for it is a *frame of reference*—a boundary within which we operate, and it therefore tends to mould our thoughts, especially if it is a restricted and restricting boundary. A child is soon initiated into a world of *good words*—' kind '; ' clean '; ' busy '; and *bad words*—' naughty '; ' dirty '; ' spiteful '; ' lazy '. See also the examples on FRAME 191 for a more advanced study of this phenomenon.

PTO FRAME 77

---

188 Communication is thus the ' carrier wave ' of the social process upon which the ' modulations ' of *knowledge, skills, beliefs* and *behaviour* are imposed in order that they may be made manifest to organize, stabilize and modify social life and transmit its essentials over space and time.

The social process, the activities of *knowing, doing, believing* and *behaving*, may be regarded as being dependent upon communication, for if we had to learn all over again the accumulated experience of the previous generations, we should *never* rise above the primitive existence —hence the saying that ' every civilization is only twenty years away from barbarism '.

PTO FRAME 189

---

300 A child who is not stimulated through communication, who does not play with other children or partake in the family's meal-time talk, may not be conscious of a deficiency in his life until he is required to communicate in a group situation which he cannot avoid—in higher education seminars or, perhaps, in management conferences.

It is at this stage that anxiety arises from the realization that he has never practised the functions and procedure of *simple* communication before being required to perform in a more complex situation. Neither has he learned to sublimate his anxieties by means of the safety-valve of personal relationships in social intercourse.

PTO FRAME 301

77 One further point—languages differ considerably in vocabulary and this is usually a reflection of differences in the physical and cultural environment. Eskimos have several words to describe different kinds of ' snow ', for their survival may depend on these fine distinctions. Arab races similarly have various words for ' sand '.

These cultural variations in vocabulary are particularly noticeable in dealings with developing countries whose physical and cultural environments contrast with ours, and serve to re-iterate the point made earlier (FRAMES 7-9, 46-51, 60, 63-64) that any phenomenon can only be communicated in terms of experiences common to both communicator and receiver.

PTO FRAME 78

---

189 In fact, since society involves—some would say ' consists of '—cooperative activity and since cooperative activity is impossible without communication, we can say, in the words of the philosopher, John Dewey, ' Society only exists by communication—and in a sense it originated in communication '.

It is very tempting to think of society, also, as a static entity, but it is really an on-going *process* like communication (FRAMES 175-179), being recreated in some vital aspect every moment through the communicative interaction of organizations, groups and, above all, individuals who constitute these units—all sharing to some degree the understanding of what is implied by a given word or action.

(**Q**) Can you list the three essential pre-requisites for a simple conversation?

PTO FRAME 190

---

301 On the contrary, however, a child may well be the subject of *excessive demands* in communication—being regarded as a potential prodigy in a bilingual home or a ' musical ' home may result in the child's plain refusal to accept the communication load, or more commonly, to simulate compliance while seeking more balanced and rewarding relationships outside the home or in a fictitious world of reading or writing or egocentric conversation.

Such compensating activities help him to look at the situation in a new light through a feed-back mechanism which may either reinforce the pathological condition or oppose and eventually correct it.

PTO FRAME 302

While reading this section, and the following section on ' Literacy and printing in modern times ', you may find it interesting and useful to consult the ' *Chronology of communication* ' which follows the end of this text.

The ancients believed that *writing* was of divine origin and in almost all non-literate societies the written word is still regarded with awe and has the force of magic. To possess another man's name in writing is to have power over him.

Probably the earliest written records in the Indo-European languages are the Vedic hymns in Sanskrit (c 2000 BC). In Ancient Egypt the hieratic script was reserved solely for religious purposes.

PTO FRAME 79

---

190 John and Bob, whom we first met in FRAME 50, are about to engage in conversation at long last—a highly civilized endeavour, one subject to several exacting conditions :

1) Before *any* communication can take place, they must share a common set of symbols (FRAMES 52, 59-65) inherited from their common culture (FRAMES 171-172).

2) The symbols used in the conversation are, for the most part, *spoken words*—their language must be learned during childhood *socialization* and improved through *education* (FRAME 85) and experience as a more or less mature person.

3) Unless the *receiver responds* to the *communicator* there is no communication—only transmission (FRAMES 5-9).

John: ' Lend me a quid '.
Bob: ' Can't—skint '.

PTO FRAME 191

---

302 Psychiatrists may often try to manipulate this mechanism in order to effect a patient's recovery, but sometimes, as in the case of the compulsive, ritualistic hand-washer, over-stimulated by parental warnings about a world drenched in ' harmful ' bacteria, the patient is virtually unapproachable, certainly not amenable to logic.

(Q) To revert to our little boy at the 'bus-stop—can you ' frame ' an appropriate response (!) If you are a parent already, perhaps you now feel apprehensive at the prospect of having to talk to *any* child *ever again*! The little boy's original question was on FRAME 294.

PTO FRAME 303

79 The existence of objective written historical records introduced the possibility of a critical scrutiny of inherited wisdom so that the past no longer had such a comprehensive hold upon the prejudices, fears and superstitions of the individual members of a literate community. Thought became more linear and logical in form and judgements more objective.

According to McLuhan, the major disaster caused by the introduction of writing was that the full and intimate world of pre-literate man's imagination was replaced to some extent by the classified ideas and logical reasoning of a literate culture at second-hand.

PTO FRAME 80

---

191 This frame might equally well have been inserted in the section on spoken language—PART 4 FRAMES 67-77—but because it has very strong associations with the cultural environment, we decided to use it as a conclusion to *this* part.

Mastery of language and communication is not always the panacea—the key to a rich life—that it might seem. Remember Caliban's retort to Prospero (Shakespeare Wm, *Tempest* Act 1 Scene 2):
' You taught me language, and my profit on't
Is that I know how to curse. The red plague rid you
For learning me your language '.
In the contemporary theatre, Peter Handke's Kaspar, though eager to learn, is disillusioned:
' I have been made to speak. I have been sentenced to reality '.—the reality, perhaps, of John and Bob.

PTO FRAME 192 FOR PART 9

---

303 Had the child been vouchsafed adequate *feedback* in the form of a clear, firm and reasoned response, even if negative in content, he would have preserved understanding and a stable relationship:
' I'm sorry, Peter, we cannot get home until the number ninety 'bus arrives, but when it *does* come, in about five minutes, we can expect to be home, warm and dry, by tea-time.

Tension is reduced, frustration is replaced by, say, constructive planning of the evening's activities and there arises an atmosphere of mutual agreement *either* to endure the cold for five minutes *or* at least, to disagree in an equally civilized and calm manner about the necessity to wait at all.

PTO FRAME 304

80 So:

Writing, especially when committed to a portable, more-or-less permanent medium such as papyrus, vellum or paper, makes it possible for man's intellectual heritage, as well as his day-to-day communication, to:

1) *Survive* without distortion or mutation over long periods of time, and:

2) Be *distributed* over the literate population of the known world in the original tongue or in translation.

(Q) One kind of institution in particular is intimately concerned with this process. What is it? What functions does it fulfil?

PTO FRAME 81

---

192 PART 9: INTER-PERSONAL COMMUNICATION—BASIC MODELS OF THE DYADIC SITUATION

Attempts have been made to capture the essence of the communication process by means of ' *models* '—replicas or charts of the ideal situation with a minimum of ' *variables* '.

We have the obvious, simple situation of the three basic elements:

SPEAKER—SPEECH—AUDIENCE

formalized as:

COMMUNICATOR—MESSAGE—RECEIVER

PTO FRAME 193

---

304 '*Agreement to disagree*' is, of course, a fundamental necessity in human relationships, as we learn to accept the referee's decision or the outcome of a debate in a democratic organization—but, of course, it can only be arrived at and conveyed by effective and free communication—which is why we propose to discuss briefly the question of ' indoctrination ' in the next few frames, especially as it affects children.

PTO FRAME 305

81 Once communication and intellectual concepts could be crystallized into tangible, portable forms for preservation and distribution, it became possible for man to store and circulate his knowledge in signs and symbols.

Libraries are stores of knowledge and even if man, through some bizarre chance, were to lose his powers of speech, he would still be able to learn from the past, communicate in the present and pass on knowledge to future generations through the medium of the written word and the library machinery for storing and circulating documents.

PTO FRAME 82

---

193 Claude Shannon and Warren Weaver: *Mathematical theory of communication* (1949), postulate a slightly more elaborate model:

SOURCE—MESSAGE—CHANNEL—RECEIVER

Take as an illustration the lecturer who wishes to explain a point to a student in a tutorial—to make the student share with him the concept that is in his (the lecturer's) mind.

1) The lecturer is the *source*.
2) His explanation, suitably encoded in symbols, is the *message*.

(Q) Can you complete the structure of this model?

PTO FRAME 194

---

305 INDOCTRINATION IN CHILDHOOD

'*Indoctrination*' is largely brought about by *selective responses* to another person who is to be indoctrinated in which one may, for example, selectively acknowledge mainly long-term or short-term prestige-winning behaviour patterns or, perhaps, symbolic actions which often become substitutes for really effective action, as when a destructive child is allowed to 'get away with' an apology, or in cases where *constructive* action is seldom adequately rewarded and communication is a succession of 'do nots' and 'must nots'.

For some details about the basic concept of the indoctrination process, turn back if you wish to FRAMES 274-275 then—

—PTO FRAME 306

82 In place of the 'wise man of the tribe', the library has become the corporate memory of a civilization. There was developed, for example, the *library of Assur-bani-pal* (668-662 BC) whose clay tablets were brought to light during the excavation of the royal palace at Nineveh during the nineteenth century AD. The library had its own staff, the books were catalogued and were arranged by subject.

PTO FRAME 83

---

194 3) The *channel* may be the sound-waves created by his voice, or the sound cassette, radio or record-player; the diagrams on the chalkboard or over-head projector, the images of the film, slide or television monitor.

4) The *receiver* is, of course, the student who decodes the message.

But note that a fifth element is often added to this model—the student will respond to the transmission of the message by nodding his head, asking a question or drumming his fingers on the table—or by some other signs of comprehension/non-comprehension, agreement/disagreement.

PTO FRAME 195

---

306 Emotional responses can become in themselves, *rewards or punishments* in this process of indoctrination, instead of remaining passive conditions of satisfaction or dissatisfaction.

Remember, for example, the humiliating dependence of the brainwashed political prisoner or prisoner-of-war upon his captors' approval of his attitudes. Remember also the conventional rewards and punishments of the more elementary programmed text which rewards you with the glowing phrase: 'Your answer is correct because . . .' or punishes you with the stark rebuff: 'You are wrong because . . .' Don't worry, though—as we said before, we're not brain washing *you*!

PTO FRAME 307

83 There was also the great Royal Library at Alexandria, and by the first century BC, the Sosii brothers of Rome were doing a flourishing trade in developing a book publishing and distribution system.

PTO FRAME 84

---

195 This *response* is technically known as *feedback* and it is of the utmost importance in communication. It enables the communicator, if he is observant and resourceful, to adjust his message or stop altogether when he gets feedback which indicates boredom, incredulity or hostility; it enables him also to monitor his tone, rate of speech, choice of language, volume and other elements of his delivery; adjust the volume control of the record player; correct his spelling on the chalk-board or the focus of the film projector.

If he does *not* scan for feedback, decode it and respond to it in his turn, he is not communicating, merely transmitting.

(Q) Construct a complete model for this situation.

PTO FRAME 196

---

307 Indoctrination is sometimes intended to produce and often results in, a similarly sterile, impersonal level of communication which militates against the flowering of *self-awareness*, the *sense of identity and rôle* which shows in late childhood and the early days of adult life and which is, in itself, a pre-requisite for participation in social communication chains. It is against this awareness that the individual can evaluate all incoming communication and because of this awareness that meaningful relationships can be established and 'mechanized' by means of outgoing communication.

PTO FRAME 308

84 In fact, you might have been tempted to quote '*publishing houses*' in answer to the previous question (FRAME 80)—and there is much to be said for your choice in this context.

We regard publishing houses as being intimately concerned with the distribution of knowledge in written form, but to have no storage, preservation or limited circulation functions beyond the short-term considerations of financial probity and to have only limited concern for the longer-term progress of the human race.

PTO FRAME 85

---

196 SOURCE (Lecturer)—encodes MESSAGE—delivers it via an appropriate CHANNEL—student is RECEIVER—he decodes and exhibits response in the form of FEEDBACK. As a SOURCE, student in turn encodes feedback MESSAGE—delivers it via an appropriate CHANNEL to RECEIVER (the lecturer this time) who decodes it and reacts in a suitable manner as the SOURCE of a new communication cycle, indicating that the feedback from the student has conditioned his attempt to communicate.

PTO FRAME 197

---

308 A similar result is often achieved when the child is made conscious that parental expectations are merely the projection of parental wishful thinking in retrospect: 'Perhaps she can get to ballet school—I wish that I had'.

But the complete absence of expectations, on the other hand, suggests exclusion from the parents' considerations and when accompanied by spasmodic shows of excessive permissiveness or generosity on their part in self-conscious over-compensation, the child's own wishful thinking propensities may be stimulated. He may adopt excessively 'grown-up' modes of communication which spill over into swearing, delinquency, addictions and other forms of conflict. Society may react by communicating only harshly, by commands, or by ignoring him.

PTO FRAME 309

85 As for the *'educational systems'* (another likely answer to the question on FRAME 80) these tend to invest directly in human talent and achievement rather than in tangible, but second-hand, records of achievement that line the shelves of libraries. However, it is true that if man, in addition to losing his power of speech (FRAME 81), were also to lose his ability to write and read, he would within a generation, exist in a time vacuum—the accumulated knowledge would be as useless as a prehistoric ritual incantation and there would be no means of passing it on to the young except, once more, by *mime*—this is not to say that society could not *exist* without universal speech and literacy, but—

PTO FRAME 86

---

197 The inter-personal communication process is a *two-way process.* To take a more homely, perhaps a more 'telling' example. (Excuse the pun—quite unintentional!)

John is again short of money—he's pretty sure that Bob is still a soft touch for a fiver and he approaches carefully this time—'I wonder if you could help me out, Bob . . . just a fiver this time . . . ?'

Bob's eyebrows knit in horror and rage—John falters on—'well, perhaps four pounds would do . . . three . . . one . . . fifty pence?'

Bob's feedback has conditioned John's request—communication might be two-way, but, apparently, lending money isn't!

PTO FRAME 198

---

309 THREATENING COMMUNICATION

Barriers to communication with others, or threats to the awareness of identity and rôle are often countered by *repressing disturbing and stressful areas of the memory* or, alternatively, by *attributing them to another 'person' in a pseudo-interpersonal relationship* in order to maintain some kind of communication link with an 'outsider', even an imagined one.

They may be similarly relegated to world of *play and fantasy* as when long and intimate conversations are held with oneself (FRAMES 34, 74-75), with a teddy-bear or with a pop-star's poster-portrait as a substitute for neglect or 'over-fussiness' by inadequate parents (FRAMES 292-304).

PTO FRAME 310

4*

86—it is both fascinating and salutary to trace the effects of communication in history and to consider the possible consequences if some developments, which we now take for granted, had not in fact taken place.

What might have been the shape of ancient, mediaeval and modern society if we had not learned to progress beyond the shouting of a message across the backyard wall or the river-boundary of our tribal territory?

PTO FRAME 87

---

198 As a last illustration of feedback and of the importance of having a two-way flow in communication, let us take the Zen Buddhist riddle:

'Is there a sound in the forest when a tree crashes down with no-one there to hear it?'

We guess that the answer is 'no'; there are sound *waves* but there can be no sound unless there is an ear to receive them, a brain to decode them (and a body to respond in some way, perhaps,—by a warning cry, an involuntary shriek of alarm or a smart sidestep!).

PTO FRAME 199

---

310 To take the matter a step further, *commands*, especially those involving *prohibitions,* are sometimes necessary for the child's protection from dangers which he is not yet sufficiently physically mature to combat successfully. Commands should not normally be given where the child's range of skills is adequate for the problem-solving involved, for they are one-way transmissions, not true communications, and are only slightly less reprehensible than the deliberate over-protection of a child or by the false appeal to his sense of 'belonging' when a parent says: 'No-one in our family would *dream* of doing that!'

A child faced with over-protection by manipulation of his environment or with the prospect of being outlawed from the family could be forgiven for breaking off communication on the spot.

PTO FRAME 311

87 To crystallize this rather vague and far-ranging enquiry:

(Q) What *three* major developments in social history have instigated the birth of literacy in a civilization—and have fostered its subsequent development?

We must remember that a 'chicken-and-egg' approach to these questions is neither useful nor enlightening. We cannot say in precisely what order these features of civilized life began to appear.

PTO FRAME 88

199 A second point worthy of note here is that we rarely communicate *in one channel only*—usually in two channels, sometimes in more. In the last, painful, episode of the John and Bob saga, John probably rolled his eyes and sighed and moaned . . . Bob probably rolled up his sleeves and snorted. John probably plucked out his empty pocket linings; Bob probably plucked his loaded wallet off the desk into the safety of his pocket. See a list of many more possibilities in FRAMES 112-127.

If John makes his request on the telephone, his personal safety is assured, but he has to rely on the inflections in Bob's voice, his changes of tone, gasps of disbelief—and that snort! A printed or typed letter would similarly employ italics, bold type, exclamation marks.

PTO FRAME 200

311 Communication within a threatening context is subject to many constraints. The threat may be directed against the personal *safety* and *integrity* of the individual, or against his *relations* with his family, peer-group or other favoured group. It may be a threat to the *conclusion of a prized endeavour* or, perhaps, against *such mandatory responses in his personality* as a jealously-guarded personal freedom of speech or action.

PTO FRAME 312

88 We would suggest:

1) Urbanization.
2) Sophisticated forms of government.
3) Systematization of the growth of knowledge in libraries.

In the first place, the influence of geographical environment and the location of natural resources were important factors in the motivation to become literate. As people travelled greater distances to trade with other communities it became important to keep records of goods bought and sold, to keep accounts, explain conditions for credit, explain delays in delivery, and so on.—

PTO FRAME 89

---

200 The *face-to-face* communication situation between *two people* is, of course, regarded as the paradigm, or ideal representation, of the *dyadic situation*. Instead of the usual metaphor of the simple telegraph circuit, it is, perhaps, better illustrated by the metaphor of the coaxial cable, with many signals flowing in parallel channels to create a multi-media communication event.

PTO FRAME 201 FOR PART 10

---

312 Similarly, it is cruel in the extreme to openly attack a person's cherished *beliefs and hopes* by means of public communication channels, more especially when *lying communication*, not usually a threat in itself, is used to create in his mind doubts as to the actual validity of those beliefs and hopes. (For an example, *see* FRAME 218.)

Threats such as these create conditions in the individual's personality ranging from rational appraisal of the threat or only mild anxiety in a relatively well-balanced person to a disabling hysterical reflex in others not so well balanced.

PTO FRAME 313

89—systems of numbers, dates, weights and measures, costs and prices evolved and people skilled in the management of these facilities tended to congregate at centres of production, growing sea-ports, frontier posts and, later, in centres of finance and investment and intelligence. *Urban life,* more or less as we know it, began to emerge.

Secondly, one may postulate a *more sophisticated system of civil administration* as city development and the conditions of city life became more complex. This would result in new local government structures, new communication systems and new strivings for a unified political identity.

PTO FRAME 90

---

201 PART IO: COMMUNICATION FROM INDIVIDUAL TO GROUP
We have already seen the problems and opportunities of the dyadic situation. Suppose now that the two individuals are joined by a third person who comes from a rather different background—say, the lecturer's eight-year-old nephew. The conversation would probably become stilted; at the risk of being ill-mannered, points which the lecturer and student could take for granted and leave unsaid, now have to be explained in detail, probably losing impact in the process.

Some psychologists believe that the conversation now becomes a ' *performance* ' in front of the newly-arrived ' audience ', with each of the principals trying to establish a degree of dominance over the other.

PTO FRAME 202

---

313 However, it is notable that ambulatory *schizophrenics,* somewhat lacking in the capacity to react in any extreme manner, often exhibit the cool rational appraisal of threatening situations which can only be matched by highly-trained persons such as air-line pilots, surgeons, boxers, some construction workers and skilled debaters.

Both categories of individuals are, to some significant degree and in their different ways, *isolated* from the threatening communication at the moment of crisis—the barriers that protect them are real, very necessary, and highly effective.

(Q) Do such persons bring a special gift to their work in the community?

PTO FRAME 314

90 It is essential that in such circumstances, orders and instructions, laws, summonses and sentences, should arrive at heavily populated and possibly remote centres in exactly the same form as that in which they were despatched and in a form in which they could be interpreted and understood by the majority of the populace.

PTO FRAME 91

---

202 The problem becomes more acute when the speaker has to address a group and the larger the group the more acute the problem. The communicator will still watch for *feedback,* but may be dismayed by its variety or its level—or by its absence among a completely passive audience (FRAMES 194-198).

There may be *physical noise* as the overhead projector hums away or a nearby road drill or fire siren intrudes—it may be the nervous jingling of coins in the lecturer's pocket or his peculiar mannerism of loping all over the platform.

Semantic noise may arise from his use of unfamiliar jargon without explanations or an unfamiliar dialect (FRAMES 156 and 166).

PTO FRAME 203

---

314 ' NEED TO COMMUNICATE '

It seems that this type of personality, commonly labelled ' schizophrenic ' tends to be *par excellence* the *withdrawn, non-participating, uncommunicative observer* of society. He often compensates for his lack of social finesse by imputing to others these very qualities which he recognizes in his own personality.

PTO FRAME 315

91 As for the *systematization of knowledge in libraries*, we have already noted (FRAME 82) that at least one major library of ancient times had its documents arranged in subject order and catalogued as a basis for study and research.

This excellent and supremely utilitarian arrangement demands as a pre-requisite, some clear consensus and pronouncement about the ' *identity*, *names* and *relationships* of the concepts which are held, at the relevant time, to comprise ' knowledge '.

PTO FRAME 92

---

203 The problems of addressing an audience form part of the study of *rhetoric*. In a classic work of the same name, Aristotle offered many suggestions in the art of persuasion—for example, he advocated the division of a discourse into three clear sections:

1) The *introduction*: ' tell 'em what you're going to tell 'em '.
2) The *argument*: ' tell 'em '.
3) *The recapitulation*: ' tell 'em what you've just told 'em '.

To the economically-minded newspaper reporter telegraphing his copy or to the Trans-Atlantic telephone caller, this may seem to be very wasteful of resources, But we have already produced an argument in favour of Aristotle's principle.

(Q) —can you name it?

PTO FRAME 204

---

315 Scientific and technological civilization has many uses for the talents of such a *detached observer* as the scientist, inventor, explorer and so on.

Living and working in an inter-acting group brings an anxiety and, sometimes, a reluctance to regard others as anything more than cyphers.

As a top-level administrator or trouble-shooter, he is relatively free of concern for them in their various personal difficulties and can be a realist in his evaluation of their influence upon him, which he usually regards as detrimental.

PTO FRAME 316

92 Once this is done, the same sequential arrangement of concepts, suitably adapted for transfer from the realm of ' pure ' knowledge, may be used for the organization and arrangement of the actual documents on shelves and for the descriptions of them which are filed in catalogues.

One prominent British librarian has described this process of ' *classification* ' as being ' itself an education '.

PTO FRAME 93

---

204 Remember *redundancy* (FRAMES 164-165)? We agreed that it could be very useful, even necessary, to re-iterate essential information in communication and, in fact, you may have noticed a good deal of redundancy in this programmed text—for example when ever we have referred you back, or forwards, to frames elsewhere in the sequence. We hope that it has proved to be useful.

One factor which redundancy can help to overcome is the limited *attention span* of the average audience. No matter now keenly they try to attend to what is being said, their attention wanders because of physical or mental fatigue or some kind of ' noise '.

PTO FRAME 205

---

316 He is often of *high intelligence*, using colourful, involved and, to some people, unintelligibly convoluted language about abstract concepts of scientific and social theory.

He remains *lonely*, as in fact he probably was in childhood, re-living in his frequently jerky and poorly-coordinated physical movements the non-verbal action language which was all he achieved in early life, when he probably also learned to regard with suspicion and alarm the ' inconsistent ' and ' devious ' communications of those around him.

PTO FRAME 317

93 All this discussion falls within the area of study known as the ' *sociology of knowledge* ' and we are approaching the outer limits of our proper territory.

Perhaps we should return to a study of the development of the written language.

(Q) Can you list *six* early forms of writing scripts? If so you should know enough about the early history of writing for our present purpose —check the list of these scripts on FRAME 94 and, if satisfied, move straight on to FRAME 100. If not, carry straight on with the text. So now, having written your list—

PTO FRAME 94

---

205 The average lecturer has been shown to grip his audience for some ten to fifteen minutes but there then ensues a steady decline in their level of attention until a small peak or surge after about fifty minutes when the speaker shuffles his notes together and says:

' Finally . . .'

The art of the good communicator lies in his ability to recapitulate the essential points of his address in such a way as to bring in the listeners whose attention had wandered while not boring those few who *were,* in fact, listening with rapt attention the first time these points were mentioned.

PTO FRAME 206

---

317 For the rest of us, inadequate and unsatisfactory communication breeds *frustration*—which stems from our inability to find a balance between, say, continuing the old conversation and the desire to introduce new, possibly unrelated, topics; between, say, the urge for self-expression and adaptation to an on-going bipartite or group situation; between our tolerance of social interaction and our desire to escape from it.

PTO FRAME 318

94 Our list reads:

1) Pictographic symbols.
2) Pictographic writing (cuneiform).
3) Ideographic representation.
4) Hieroglyphics.
5) Demotic script.
6) Alphabets - Phoenician, Hebrew, Greek . . .

Pictographic symbols—the first complete series of symbolic records may date back as much as 40,000 years and we know that by 20,000 BC man was drawing images on the walls of the caves at Altamira, in Spain.

PTO FRAME 95

---

206 This raises the important question of the careful structuring of the content of a talk. Keypoints may be emphasized by being grouped at the beginning of the talk, considered at length in the middle section and then re-iterated during a final summing up—the *climactic device*.

Vocal variety can emphasize the points by changes in the rate, pitch, inflection and articulation of the delivery because we hear words not in a strictly logical linear sequence of letters, phonemes and morphemes (see FRAME 157) but in patterns of sound that convey the ideas. A secretary taking dictation or a wireless operator reading fairly fast Morse code do not deal with the messages letter-by-letter but tend to pause, waiting for a complete ' *semantic unit* ' before moving ahead with the appropriate response.

PTO FRAME 207

---

318 The fault may lie in ourselves or in our correspondents but the resulting tension and restlessness may permanently sour a relationship and lead to a sense of *isolation* in both social and intellectual dimensions. Is this evidence of the so-called ' *need to communicate* '?

We do not know that isolation is necessarily a traumatic experience for the majority, but we *do* know that in some cases at least, it can lead to breakdown or even death.

PTO FRAME 319

95 Although, strictly, this was pre-writing and although there may have been more ritual magic about it than any conscious attempt at communication, yet from these cave-dwellers came early attempts to string together a series of pictorial representations of objects, ie, *pictograms,* to represent a train of thought.

These pictograms were of a distinctly different nature to their precursors—the Wampum belts of some American Indians and the knotted cords of prehistoric northern Europe, for example.

PTO FRAME 96

---

207 Aristotle defined *rhetoric* as ' the search for all available means of persuasion '. Since librarians are in the communication and persuasion game, let us imagine Joe Bloggs, ALA, freshly minted from library college and faced with the task of whipping up local enthusiasm for a new branch library that is making a rather slow start.

He is required to address local groups on the ideals and objectives of the service and on the practical advantages accruing to those who join and use the branch regularly.

(Q) Try to adduce *ten* criteria from the foregoing frames by which his performance might be judged.

PTO FRAME 208

---

319 TIMING OF COMMUNICATION

We also know, of course, that temporary isolation of relatively short duration can be a *healing influence* for some, especially in moments of crisis and that in those circumstances the use of communication facilities in addressing them must be *carefully timed.*

Just as society has its working day and its leisure hours and just as shift-work far into the night disrupts large segments of social life outside the place of work—shopping, sex-life, entertainment, eating and sleeping, so the human being, especially the disturbed human being, has daily and monthly biological rhythms.

(Q) Do you know of longer-term rhythms in human life?

PTO FRAME 320

96 A later development was *pictographic writing*—a wedge-shaped script devised by the Sumerians and known as *cuneiform*. It was in use in what is now southern Iraq in the fourth millennium BC and was still representational in intent—the sun was shown by a circle; a man was shown by a formalized reclining silhouette.

PTO FRAME 97

---

208 1) How does he see his purpose and define the favourable *mental set* which he hopes to instil? (FRAMES 46-47)

2) How does he assess the *needs and probable interests* of the different audiences he meets—businessmen, school children, Women's Institute members, church groups? (FRAMES 134, 157, 162-163, 214, 224-228)

3) How does he adjust his *choice of concepts, language and examples* to these audiences? (FRAMES 48, 50, 62-64, 76, 135-148)

4) How does he propose to *structure his address*—should he play his trump cards in the introduction, plod unimaginatively through them in the middle, or keep them to the end and risk 'losing' the audience? (FRAME 206)

PTO FRAME 209

---

320 We know of annual cycles in road deaths and suicides and attempted suicides and we know of the unexplained forty-one month cycle of business activity.

To some limited extent these may be evidence of obscure communication systems, in that, for example, road behaviour may be to some extent expressive of temperament or personality changes; a suicide may be an unsuccessful, because unanswered, call for help; a business slump may be the expression of corporate lapses of confidence.

PTO FRAME 321

97 The next stage in development was the *ideographic*—in that the circle came to suggest not only ' sun ' but also other associated concepts—' heat ', ' day ', ' time '.

There was, as yet, no connection between the *ideographic symbol* and the *sound of the spoken word*—but there was one major advantage in this situation.

(Q) Have you any idea as to the nature of this advantage?

PTO FRAME 98

209

5) Does he use *vocal variety* to emphasize his points? (FRAME 206)

6) Does his *delivery* suggest that he is closeted with a solitary, rather sick, listener or that he is haranguing a crowd? (FRAME 134)

7) Does he display warmth and concern or is he formal, distant and icily impartial in his use of *body language*? (FRAMES 123-126)

8) Does he *observe the rules of social communication* to secure attention, understanding and acceptance? (FRAMES 184-186)

9) Does he *eliminate noise*? (FRAME 166)

10) Does he promote *helpful redundancy*? (FRAMES 164-165, 203-205)

11) Does he *make use of feedback*? (FRAMES 195-198)

PTO FRAME 210

---

321 It is possible, therefore, that communication with a tired, hungry, suicidal business woman, driving over a high suspension bridge at night on the 19th May 197– might just be the last straw in a disturbed relationship, especially if you have been unable to ' prepare ' her for the bad news about her firm's chances of survival and if the three people in the back of the car are arguing loudly about football at the same time.

(Q) What does this rather extreme example teach us about the essentials of communication in already difficult circumstances?

PTO FRAME 322

98 Not until much later did the ideographic symbol come to denote not only an object or quality or activity but also the sound associated with it. *In the meantime—the written language could be understood by people who spoke mutually unintelligible dialects.*

Near the end of the third millennium BC the Sumerian civilization declined but its cuneiform ideographic script was taken over and spread successively by the Assyrians, Babylonians and Persians.

Parallel with this development of cuneiform, the Egyptians developed their *hieroglyphics* (literally, ' sacred carvings ') which gradually evolved into a more cursive form known as ' *demotic* '.

PTO FRAME 99

---

210 *Appeals* which Joe could make to his audiences are based on the arts of the professional persuaders:

1) *Social* appeal: *Everybody* uses the library!
2) *Prestige* appeal: *All the best people* use the library!
3) *Survival* appeal: *No one can compete* in modern life without help from the library!
4) *Fun* appeal: Use the library for *fun and leisure*!
5) *Egomaniac* appeal: Knowledge is *power*!
6) *Fear* appeal: If you don't use the library your friends will *ostracize you*!

PTO FRAME 211

---

322 *Timing, preparation* and a proper appreciation of the *context* by all concerned are vital to successful communication. If they are neglected and especially if irrelevant and hurtful *extraneous matter* is introduced into the message, the barriers will drop into place between individuals and society will lose cohesion and impetus.

PTO FRAME 323

99 The first true sound-and-meaning-consistent *alphabet* was formed by the Phoenicians some time before 1500 BC and contained 22 letters. Since the Phoenicians were great travellers and traders, and since their alphabet was devised in part at least for trading purposes (see FRAMES 87-90 again for the implications of this), it was implanted in many countries and used in modified forms, for example, by the Hebrews to write down the Old Testament stories and by the Greeks to record their literature, philosophy and science. From the Greeks it has descended in a virtually unbroken line to modern times.

(Q) Can you think of the invention behind the *next* major phase of civilized communication?

PTO FRAME 100

---

211 MEDIA OF MASS COMMUNICATION

With the advent of mass communication facilities, whole populations felt the power of the new media to *persuade* people to adopt certain courses of action or certain attitudes as they were propagated.

The mass media are distinguished by their ability to reach *all classes of a population,* directly or indirectly, within a *relatively brief span of time*—a few days or even hours—with a message that represents the *lowest common denominator of comprehension* in that population.

The mass media commonly work on the assumption that each individual is completely *passive* and will accept the communication like an injection—the ' *magic bullet* ' theory of persuasion.

PTO FRAME 212

---

323 THE PATHOLOGY OF GROUP COMMUNICATION

FRAMES 221-275 (PARTS 11 and 12) deal with the problems of group communication in *normal* circumstances, but:

Special considerations arise in connection with the pathological aspects of group communications. In this situation, for even a minimum level of efficiency, the flow of messages must be particularly well-organized, the language must be common to all participants and the underlying assumptions of the group outlook must be fully appreciated and approved by all. Since one person's inefficiency or defection may disrupt the whole network, members are expected to exercise *restraint,* endure *tensions* and even *make sacrifices* for the group.

PTO FRAME 324

This next major step in the development of communication by language occurred in Western Europe, even in its embryonic forms, less than a thousand years ago, although there had been rumours of its establishment as a novel and limited technique in the Far East at a somewhat earlier date. As with so many of our ' modern ' inventions, current research is revealing Chinese antecedents in the technology of communications.

PTO FRAME IOI

---

212 In fact, it is comforting to realize that the individual is much more complex than this, with a whole constellation of attitudes and batteries of deflector shields to protect him from forcefully expressed contrary opinion from without.

The mass communicator suffers even greater disadvantages than Joe Bloggs ALA, for the process of *mass* communication is much more complex than a mere address to a luncheon club.

Instead of an individual communicator, the mass media are generally manipulated by large organizations, perhaps a nationalized corporation, with elaborate plant and hierarchical management structure (for *their* problems of communication see PART 12 FRAMES 233-275!). Messages may originate from within the organization or equally within governmental or commercial concerns with varying degrees of authority over the media.

PTO FRAME 213

---

324 On the other hand, where a member is known to be eccentric or suffering from some pathological condition that may threaten the group's corporate communication network, he may be *ostracized* if he genuinely cannot or will not adapt to group norms.

It may be, however, that his deviation is *not* evidence of his own maladjustment but rather a symptom of some *group disturbance*. It may be necessary then to treat the group network as a whole, just as a child's delinquency may signal the communication inadequacies of his whole family.

PTO FRAME 325

101 In the fifteenth century AD a third phase in human communication began with the re-invention and elaboration of the *printing press* by Johannes Gutenberg: the press not only copied words mechanically but did it with impressive speed and in a potentially limitless number of copies. What would the enterprising Sosii brothers of Rome (FRAME 83) have made of this device?

Of course, like most 'inventions', it emerged as an answer to a pressing and long-established *need* for during the previous two centuries more than fifty of Europe's great universities had been founded and university-based book-copying establishments had been unable to cope with the demand for manuscript documents.

PTO FRAME 102

---

213 As suggested before (FRAME 211), the audience of the mass media is vast and heterogeneous with widely differing values, education and social background.

Feedback from this audience is normally received by post or telephone or in the press and is usually too late to influence the programme by the time advice has filtered through the 'official' channels of communication within the organization.

Only very recently has it been possible to provide at great cost and with very elaborate techniques, a measure of immediate, if formally-structured feedback by telephone directly to the programme while it is in progress.

Gillian Reynolds, *Guardian* newspaper critic, 17th February 1973, described the process of this feedback operation as 'like being on a crossed line and hearing someone else's conversation. It makes you . . . very nervous and trembly '.

PTO FRAME 214

---

325 The foundations of group communication are commonly learned in the *nuclear family* in which a basic three- or four-person unit of father, mother and child(ren) gives a *greater variety of communication experience* than the two-person unit, say of the one-parent family, but a *richer emotional life* than that of the larger ' gang ' or working unit or recreational group or commune, whose various standards and objectives, unless carefully coordinated, may well clash with those of the family and cause anxiety and restricted communication if the individual thinks well of his family, or guilt and restricted communication if he does not.

(Q) Can you name some familiar ' institutions ' of social life that might induce anxiety or guilt in this way?

PTO FRAME 326

102 This new technique for the rapid reproduction of documents in multiple copies gave a tremendous impetus to the development of science and technology—the findings of one investigator could be disseminated with reasonable ease and speed to many others working in the same subject area and the, by now familiar, *knowledge-communication spiral* was given a decisive impetus through books, periodicals and learned societies in the sixteenth and seventeenth centuries.

As printed books grew in numbers and became more widely available, more people felt impelled to learn to read and write—the possibility of scholarship was extended to a wider spectrum of the population and more people were able to contribute their more varied talents to the development of the practical applications of *technology*.

PTO FRAME 103

---

214 Normally, however, the mass communicator remains blissfully unaware that Dad has put his boots on and gone to the pub and the more that theorists delve into the effects of mass communication, the more they find the same resistance to change that we saw in the case of inter-personal communication—people take from *any* communication only what they *need*, not what the communicator intends them to have. If he's on the spot he can, perhaps, do something about it: if he's remote, he's pretty helpless (see also FRAMES 14-16, 104-108).

PTO FRAME 215

---

326 Marriage, migration, confirmation into a church, a change of employment or of friends may produce similar reactions in certain circumstances but will at least introduce the younger person into a very useful experience of diversity in opinions and communication networks.

PTO FRAME 327

103 By the mid-eighteenth century the *Industrial Revolution* was in top gear in Great Britain and was firmly under way in other countries of Western Europe. At first based on *water-power*, it later involved *coal-fired steam power* that, applied to the printing presses, made books, periodicals, and newspapers more widely, and far more cheaply, available to the literate population that was required by the new industrial society. Even the humblest operative should be able to read operating instructions and safety notices, if nothing else, while the best operatives were deeply involved in research and development. It is, however, remarkable that for the previous three hundred and fifty years the printing presses had remained unchanged, as first introduced to Europe.

PTO FRAME 104

---

215 *Persuasion through opinion leaders*

It has been suggested before (FRAMES 207-211) that communication is often intended to *persuade* people to adopt some course of action or some attitude. But individuals are all members of at least one social group, usually many, and each individual tends to value highly group opinions of actions and attitudes—especially his own!

When fear of the forces of persuasion was investigated by Elihu Katz and Paul Lazarsfeld, they found that influences from the mass media reached the mass audience through *opinion leaders* or '*influentials*'— persons of prestige in their various groups—in a *two-step flow,* often in further steps.

(Q) Can you think of an important and legitimate use which can be made of this phenomenon.

PTO FRAME 216

---

327 Most people with pathological irregularities of their communication functions as described above, are characterized by an inability to *participate effectively in groups* and by a reversion to, or a failure to emerge from more or less unsatisfactory patterns of childhood communication within an inadequate family situation. Many, in fact, are crippled in communication terms by a childhood spent in a one-parent household where there has been no practice in group communication.

PTO FRAME 328

104 Emerging from this phase of the Industrial Revolution was a secondary phase, soon to assume overwhelming importance—the *Electrical/Electronic Revolution*. The range of the human voice was extended by the telegraph, telephone and radio. It became possible to stimulate the human eye across time and space by *photography, wire-transmission of photographs, moving films* and, more recently, by pictures which move concurrently with the originating events—*television*, off-air, closed circuit and cable.

PTO FRAME 105

---

216 In some developing countries, persuasion in good and vital causes such as agricultural improvement, hygiene, family planning, will be far more effective if it is directed first at *opinion leaders* or '*influentials*' in the community, or at *reference groups* such as professional societies, local councils, church congregations, who are similarly held in universal esteem. (see also FRAME 107).

Advertisers know this well and use *prestige suggestion* in their campaigns—as indeed, we recommended to Joe (FRAME 210).

PTO FRAME 217

---

328 In many groups communication networks are *over-loaded,* often with irrelevant information. A large firm selects executives who know how to delegate work, report-writers who know how to evaluate and condense information and trouble-shooting teams who can unravel knotted lines of communication and command.

PTO FRAME 329

105 In the periodical, ' *Wireless world* ' for October 1945, Arthur C Clarke predicted a further, possibly the ultimate development—the use of *artificial earth satellites*, travelling in precisely calculated orbits, as relay stations to project telephone, radio and television communications to any point on earth. It was this accelerated pace of development in communications technology, if not this particular item, that led McLuhan to speak of contemporary society as ' *the global village* '.

(Q) Can you think of one great advantage which the systems of communication mentioned in this and the previous frame, have over the written and printed word?

PTO FRAME 106

---

217 *Selective exposure and selective perception* are not *quite* what you might imagine!

It has been found by some investigators that individuals tend to *expose themselves selectively* only to communications which are in general accordance with their established convictions and to avoid especially any channel which seems to challenge their more precariously-held beliefs.

If, by accident, they are exposed to contrary, forceful, unsympathetic opinions they are able, perhaps unconsciously to *perceive selectively* in order to invest these hostile arguments with acceptable meanings, thus narrowing the gap between what they believe already and what they are invited to believe.

PTO FRAME 218

---

329 Such persons are, needless to say, engaged only in ' *station-to-station* ' calls between managers, secretaries, ministers, organizers and other impersonal rôle-holders, as opposed to the ' *person-to-person* ' calls which bear the emotional overtones of unique living relationships between these same people as friends, lovers, members of a family and bridge-partners.

Conflict arises within either type of group when modes of communication *appropriate to the other type of group* are introduced inadvertently or through miscalculation of the context (FRAMES 258-259).

PTO FRAME 330

106 The telephone, radio, photographs, film and television are all means of communication that do not rely on any special ability in reading and writing—they are, in this respect, a step back towards the primeval society of personal contact across the backyard wall or the boundary river (FRAME 86) or in the Forum or in the courtyard of the chief's kraal (FRAME 67).

The disaster predicted by McLuhan (FRAME 79) may well be averted and he may well find it necessary to postulate a fourth phase of human communication history to add to the three listed on FRAME 66.

PTO FRAME 107

---

218 We all hope very much that our deeply held beliefs may be held inviolate and *consonant* for the rest of our days. We do our best to reduce *dissonance*—in fact, this behavioural phenomenon is known as *cognitive dissonance* (FRAMES 311-312).

The story is told of the pious Irish lady who saw with horror her parish priest making his way into the town's house of ill-repute. She later argued away the dissonance by asserting roundly to her friends that he had no doubt gone in to pray with the village football team since they were more often in *there* than they were in church, and obviously destined to stay at the bottom of the league anyway without the priest's special attention!

PTO FRAME 219

---

330 Similarly, group tensions arise when there are obvious *discrepancies between claimed rôles and those which actually obtain within the group* as when a father who claims to be, or is claimed by his wife to be, honest, sober and successful in business, is known by his children to be a drunk who has to resort to fraudulent conversion of the cricket club funds to make ends meet.

Double standards of behaviour towards members of the in-group, as opposed to outsiders, or towards the group leaders, as opposed to rank-and-file members, are also disturbing and may be calculated to arouse resentment and conflict and to inhibit or distort meaningful communication.

PTO FRAME 331

107 A factor of supreme importance in developing countries is the *radio* which, through the medium of a central broadcasting station and the ubiquitous cheap transistor set, can bring information, education and a sense of identity to a national or racial, if not yet a ' global ', village. The use of the term ' *broadcast* ' brings back an old and familiar image from the more primitive, pre-technological days—the image of the *sower* who cast the seed abroad, as opposed to dribbling it thinly down the throat of the technologically advanced tractor-drawn drill. See also FRAMES 14-16, 211-214 before you—

PTO FRAME 108

---

219 *Persuasion in debate*

It can be difficult enough to communicate persuasively when you have the field to yourself, but most of us have taken part in debates at some time or other—in fact, in a democracy this forms an important element of the process of government.

Suppose that Joc had been placed in a *debate* on library use, in opposition to the local representative of the 'Association for the Abolition of Public Libraries '. His problem would now take on a new perspective.

Should he go in to bat first on the basis that ' first impressions count ' *or* should he go in last, since ' it's the *last* word that lingers in the donkey's ear.'? This principle is known rather more pompously as the ' *primacy versus recency* ' argument.

PTO FRAME 220

---

331 Individuals and their groups are interdependent to a considerable degree. As we have seen, a *sick individual* may be regarded as threatening the integrity of the group and may be removed from it against his will, or may equally be kept in it against his wishes in order to preserve a facade of group unity.

A *sick group* will usually seek to restrain a healthy individual from leaving, fearful of losing his services and his morale-building influence and equally resentful of his propaganda when he leaves to join a healthier group.

(Q) What would you recommend if consulted in such a crisis by an ailing football club?

PTO FRAME 332

108 Perhaps it is tempting fate to speak of an ' ultimate development ' (FRAME 105). Even now the science of *cybernetics* and the use of the *computer* are beginning to turn man into one half of a *man-machine interface*—and for the first time man is communicating on virtually equal terms with something other than his own kind in a non-anthropomorphic image.

PTO FRAME 109

---

220 Should he give a heavily biassed presentation on the model of the ' party political broadcast ' or should he attempt to give a balanced viewpoint and risk presenting gratuitous points to his opponent?

Experimental studies would suggest the following advice :

1) The balanced presentation has more effect *in the long run* if the audience tend to be sceptical and if they are to be subjected to counter-arguments later—more still if they are well-educated.

2) The biassed presentation can be most effective if the audience share the views of the speaker, are not going to be immediately exposed to counter-arguments—and if their educational achievement is generally low.

So there you are, Joe—go in and win!

PTO FRAME 221 FOR PART II

---

332 In most cases such as these, communication tends to be *distorted* rather than completely cut off and such distortion may persist for *long periods* before the affected individuals of the group finally acknowledge that the harm done to their relationships is probably irreparable without outside professional help.

On the other hand, a *clean break* would have left the ground clear for a fresh start in communication, beneficial to all, as when a football team with low morale is rejuvenated by a new manager, a selection of new players in key positions and a consequent change of tactics and image.

But . . .

PTO FRAME 333

109 Although this survey (FRAMES 78-108) *and* the selected list of communication landmarks in the ' Chronology of communication ' at the end of this text, may seem to cover a very long period of history, this period is in fact a dramatically limited section of man's existence on this planet.

R M McIver, the sociologist, offers the following model: If we take a twelve-hour clock face to represent the total period of man's existence on earth, each hour would represent about 40,000 years. The cave drawings at Altamira appear at 11.30; cuneiform script at 11.45; the Greek alphabet at 11.56½; and Gutenberg's printing press at 11.59¼!

PTO FRAME 110

---

221 PART II : GROUP MOTIVATION AND COHESION

Human motivation and needs are an essential background to an understanding of group communicative behaviour. If a motor mechanic loses patience with the car he's repairing, hurls the carburettor on the floor and calls the car a ' b— ole crock ', we might justifiably assess him as incompetent and unreliable and refuse to employ him again. But perhaps we should not do this until we have measured his competence in normal circumstances and investigated openly and impartially his needs, motivations and general background of poverty, nagging wife, large family, unfriendly neighbours, and so on.

We must *try* to understand *why* some people are abrasive, aggressive and uncooperative before we can understand the problems of group communication.

PTO FRAME 222

---

333 . . . if the clean break involves the *isolation* of the sick individual or group, it is often disastrous from the point of view of the chronically sick ' patient '.

Although regarded by most outsiders as the best course of action for all concerned, it may be a subterfuge, conscious or unconscious, to remove from the scene the visible evidence of ' failure '.

The incidental by-product is, of course, the disruption of the ' patient's ' communication life-line to normality and the delaying or denial of any hope of recovery and re-integration.

You might be well-advised *not* to venture an opinion on the matter!

PTO FRAME 334

110 If we view the rate of change in terms of generations, the 'communication revolution' is fantastically faster than the rate of change during the Industrial Revolution in the British Isles. A person now aged seventy years has in fact spent the greater part of his adult life without having a radio in his home, but he has also lived to see and hear man on the moon and his sons and daughters, now middle-aged, have not known life without radio and his grandchildren have had television every day of their lives unless brought up in genuine poverty.

PTO FRAME 111

---

222 Sometimes a person's motives are external and transparent (a touch of synaesthesia here—FRAME 127)—as when he puts on his coat to go out into the rain. Another man might take *off* his coat to go out into the rain if, for example, he's testing a 'shrink-proof' shirt for a television commercial.

Psychologists tend to interpret motivation as a state or condition within a person which can be regarded as a cause of complex behaviour or which can at least make it possible for us to hazard an explanation as to why different individuals react in different ways to the same situation. *Need* is a powerful motive for action.

PTO FRAME 223

---

334 A specialized type of small-group situation involves the '*symbiotic team*' in which, typically, two persons adopt interdependent rôles, expressing the dependence of one upon the other or of each upon the other. This happens especially in such closed situations as a sheltered childhood, marriage or chronic sickness in which the giving and receiving of approval or even the mutual reduction of tension by the *licensed* expression of hostility are valuable safety valves to disturbed minds isolated from outside communication.

Such a situation may also arise between an individual and a major group such as a welfare or counselling agency.

PTO FRAME 335

111

(Q) What remains, then, of our survey of the various modes of language?

PTO FRAME 112

---

223 We have already discussed briefly man's *biological needs* for food, drink, shelter, sex and rest and we have stressed that man is also a social animal (FRAMES 180-185).

Man must also, therefore, have *social needs* in so far as he depends upon his fellows.

(Q) Try to name *six* of these important social needs which become apparent when people congregate in groups.

PTO FRAME 224

---

335 Separation of such partners would represent yet another source of stress since they are rarely concerned with communication from the 'outside' and they tend to anticipate that any which is imposed upon them will, by definition, be 'harmful'.

Individuals often react to such anticipated or actual interference by resorting to drink or drugs or delinquency to counter the sense of loss by the acquisition of a substitute identity in a new 'community'.

PTO FRAME 336

People may communicate with each other without using words, spoken, written or printed, for there are many ways of offering clues as to one's attitude to the receiver, to the discourse, to the subject and even to oneself. It is possible to deal in subtleties and nuances that word-dominated modes cannot convey, as you may remember if you are old enough to remember the silent movie films—or young enough to enjoy the current revival of interest in these ' golden oldies '.

TURN BACK NOW TO FRAME 113 ON THE CENTRE SECTION OF THE FIRST PAGE OF THIS PROGRAMMED TEXT.

---

224 Some important *social needs* of the group-member are:

1) The need to *belong* to a group and share in its communication.

2) The corresponding need for a degree of *independence* within the group.

3) The need for emotional and economic *security*.

4) The corresponding need for *new experiences*.

5) The need for innovative *success* and *appreciation* by others.

6) The corresponding need for traditional *stable values*.

Of course, these needs overlap and may be sub-divided into many component drives but anybody who is entrusted with the care and supervision of people in groups must take account of them. They also figure in the calculations of the ' persuaders ' (FRAMES 210-216).

TURN BACK NOW TO FRAME 225 ON THE LOWER SECTION OF THE FIRST PAGE OF THIS PROGRAMMED TEXT.

---

336 Distant though this may seem from the normal day's work of the professional librarian, one murmurs: ' There, but for the grace of God, go I ', and one should prepare in both professional and private life, to communicate with the isolate and respond to his halting confidences.

In our capacity as managers of communication we should look with compassion on those less resourceful and less practised than ourselves who are so universally ' communicated at ', but so seldom ' communicated with '.

THE END

—BUT PTO FOR FOLLOW-UP MATERIALS

A CHRONOLOGY OF COMMUNICATIONS

The following list shows some important dates in the development of communications. No doubt, you can think of others which you consider to be more important than many of those listed here but we have tried to keep our list within reasonable proportions and to exclude any suggestion of a biassed point of view while yet suggesting the most outstanding landmarks.

Inevitably, the majority of entries are for the nineteenth and twentieth centuries because the technological discoveries of these last two hundred years have outnumbered and out-shone those of the rest of recorded history in most respects. See also PARTS 4 and 5 of the program for supplementary details and connecting links with intellectual and social aspects of communication. Few inventions happen in a vacuum but usually result from the deficiencies and needs in currently available facilities. In this connection, *see* FRAMES 100-108 for the emergence of an important invention ('re-invention' would be a more accurate term) and a case-study of the consequences and of the chain of other developments in which it was directly or indirectly involved.

In the following list most of the developments noted are strictly technological innovations, designed for, or in some cases merely applied to, the field of communication_ and communications_ (remember FRAMES 10-17?).

They have been categorized by initial letter prefixes as follows:
A—Archaeological discoveries in communication.
B—Books and scrolls.
F—Film and photography.
L—Libraries.
N—Newspapers and periodicals.
P—Printing and paper-making.
R—Radio, telephone and other voice-modes.
T—Television.
W—Writing, scripts and alphabets.

W	40,000 BC	Approximate date of earliest cave-drawings and paintings.
W	3,500 BC	Sumerians developed pictographic writing—cuneiform.
W	3,100 BC	Date of the earliest known Egyptian hieroglyphics.
W	2,500 BC	Egyptians began to develop cursive hieratic script.
P	„	Egyptians began to use papyrus.

W	2,000 BC	Vedic hymns written in Sanskrit.
W	1,800 BC	Babylonian cuneiform literature on clay tablets. Hammurabi's code of law inscribed on a stele.
W	1,700 BC	Minoans developed a script on Crete.
W	1,600 BC	Semites developed an alphabet, later transmitted by the Phoenicians.
B	1,580–1,350 BC	Egyptian 'Book of the dead', considered to be the world's first book.
W	800 BC	Etruscans adopted the Greek alphabet and transmitted it to the Romans.
B	,,	'Iliad' and 'Odyssey' written.
W	700 BC	Egyptian demotic script for secular writings.
L	668–662 BC	Library of Assur-bani-pal established in Nineveh.
L	540 BC	Foundation of the world's first public library, in Athens by Pisistratus.
W	350 BC	All the Greek states adopted twenty-four letter alphabet.
L	304–300 BC	Royal Alexandrian library established.
N	131 BC	Acta Diurna—Roman official announcements—first forerunner of the newspaper press.
W	100 BC	Roman alphabet attained its final twenty-three letter form.
B	,,	Sosii brothers established a publishing business in Rome.
N	59 BC	Julius Caesar ordered publication of Acta Senatus—official record of the senate debates.
L	48 AD	Alexandrian library destroyed for the first time.
B	150 AD	Parchment first folded into pages to make books as opposed to scrolls.
L	391 AD	Alexandrian library destroyed for the second time.
P/B	868 AD	First complete printed book—'Diamond Sutra'—now in the British Museum.
P	1221 AD	Chinese developed moveable wooden type blocks for printing.
L	1373 AD	Charles V opened what is now the Bibliothèque Nationale, the national library of France.
P	1450 AD	Johannes Gutenberg of Mainz developed both moveable type and the printing press.
P	1476 AD	William Caxton set up the first printing press in England.

N	1500 AD	Handwritten newsletters or circulars appeared.
N	1513 AD	First English newsbook told of the Battle of Flodden Field.
N	1702 AD	'Daily courant', the first English daily newspaper, appeared in London on 1st March.
N	1785 AD	'Daily universal register', first issued by John Walters.
N	1788 AD	'Daily universal register' renamed 'The Times'.
P	1799 AD	Lithography perfected by Alois Senefelder.
A	,,	Discovery of the Rosetta stone led to the deciphering of Egyptian hieroglyphics.
P	1803 AD	Development of continuous-manufacture process for paper.
P	1814 AD	'The Times' operated the first steam-powered press—1,100 newsheets per hour.
F	1822 AD	Niepce made the first photograph.
F	1837 AD	Daguerre invented a system for developing images on metal plates.
F	1841 AD	Fox-Talbot invented the negative/positive photographic process.
P	1845 AD	Richard Hoe perfected his rotary press—8,000 copies per hour.
A	1846 AD	Henry Rawlinson described cuneiform inscriptions on the Behistian Rock in Iran.
N	1851 AD	Reuter's news service opened.
R	1858 AD	First trans-atlantic cable laid.
R	1865 AD	Clerk-Maxwell's 'Electro-magnetic theory of light'.
R	1878 AD	Thomas Edison developed the cylindrical phonograph.
F	1884 AD	George Eastman invented the roll film.
P	1887 AD	Tolbert-Lanston invented the monotype machine.
R	1889 AD	Edward Branly invented the coherer (later applications were in radio).
R	1895 AD	Marconi transmitted radio signals for one mile.
F	,,	Georges Méliès founded the first moving film company.
N	1896 AD	Lord Northcliffe founded the 'Daily Mail'—prototype of the popular cheap newspaper.
R	1901 AD	Marconi transmitted radio signals across the Atlantic.
R	1904 AD	Sir John Fleming invented the vacuum tube (radio valve).
R	1920 AD	Radio station KDKA Pittsburgh opened.
R	,,	Broadcasts from Chelmsford, England, started.

R	1922 AD	British Broadcasting Company (later 'Corporation') opened at Savoy Hill, London.
T	1923 AD	Invention of the ionoscope and kinescope, for respectively transmitting and receiving television images.
F	1926 AD	Warner Brothers produced the first sound moving film with music—'Don Juan'.
F	1927 AD	First 'talkie' moving film produced—Al Jolson in 'The Singing Fool'.
R	,,	Transatlantic telephone services started.
T	1933 AD	John Logie Baird transmitted silhouettes by television.
T	1936 AD	BBC transmitted scheduled television service.
R/T	1948 AD	Invention of the transistor by Professor Shockley, USA, as replacement for the vacuum tube.
P	1950 AD	Introduction of computer type-setting.
A	1952 AD	Michael Ventris and John Chadwick deciphered the Creto-Mycenaean script, Linear B.
R/T	1960 AD	First communications laser produced in USA.
R/T	1962 AD	First direct television contact between USA and Europe, by means of Telstar satellite, which also carried radio, telephone and other communications circuits.
R	1963 AD	Unmanned space probe Mariner III established radio contact with earth over a distance of thirty-six million miles.
P	,,	Americans name the era of electronic computers the 'Intellectronic Age'. One of these machines can, for example, transmit the twenty-four volumes of the Encyclopaedia Britannica in three minutes.
R/T	1967 AD	First radio and television contact with men on the moon.

POST TEST — QUESTIONS

1 What is ' communication ' after all?
   How does it differ from ' communications '?
2 Do you believe now that man is superior to the animals in the way he manipulate the evidence presented by his senses? In what ways is he ' different ' from the animals in this respect?
3 In what different ways can we manipulate our perceptions?
4 What is ' language '?
5 Is the ' meaning ' of a word or phrase in one's own language intrinsically understandable and precise?
6 What does language do, apart from merely applying labels to objects and ideas?
7 Briefly describe the changes which ' writing ' brings to the life of primitive men.
8 Briefly describe what further changes were brought about by the introduction of printing.
9 How did the next great advance in communication technology throw us back five hundred years?
10 How would you attempt to communicate without words?
11 Briefly define: ' Information '; ' Entropy '; ' Redundancy '; ' Noise '.
12 Why is it wrong to regard ' knowledge ' and ' information ' as synonymous terms?
13 What do you mean by the term ' Informatics '?
14 Compile a brief list of ' Rules for communication '.
15 Some people ' communicate ', some merely ' transmit '. What are the differences in the two procedures?
16 How would you plan an address to a small group on a subject of your own choice?
17 What are the particular problems of the mass communicator?
18 What are the social needs that bring the members of a group to communicate with each other?
19 Why is a hierarchy a more efficient context for communication than other types of group?
20 What effect do ' rôle expectations ' have on group communication?

21 Describe or sketch *three* basic types of communication net.
22 What are the essential *factors* in successfully communicating a message, *as opposed to the constituents of a network?*
23 Define the term ' Indoctrination '.
24 What are the *seven* major barriers to communication?
25 What is meant by the term ' symbiotic team ' in the discussion of communication?

ANSWERS TO POST TEST

Again, as with the pre-test answers, we can only offer 'likely' answers to questions such as these, which deal with conceptual and subjective, rather than factual and objective matters. However, you should be able to find in your answers concepts similar to those in italics below. Give yourself one mark for each comparable concept which you have listed on your answer sheet. The act of assessing 'comparability' of answers is in itself an important part of the learning process, especially now that you have some knowledge of the subject.

1   *Imparting, conveying, exchange* of *knowledge, ideas etc. Transfer of thoughts, etc* (FRAME 5).
    Symbols of the mind and *means of conveying them* (FRAME 6).
    All the *processes whereby one mind may affect another* (FRAME 7).
    Communications refers to the *technical devices* involved (FRAMES 10-17).

2   Man is, we believe, unique in *thinking, learning, remembering and communicating* the evidence which his senses present.
    He can *compare, generalize, abstract* and *reason* (FRAMES 19, 31).
    He has created a second, symbolic, world of language (FRAME 55).

3   We perceive only 'signs' and build from them our own *symbolic pictures of the world*. *Sensory deprivation* can change behaviour. *Selective perception* leads us to miss many things in our environment. Our senses may be deceived by mental sets (FRAMES 41-50).

4   Language is a series of *signs* and *symbols* used by man for *communication*. This, however, is only one of the uses of language and language is only one of the vehicles of communication (FRAMES 52, 58).

5   The language code has no intrinsic meaning but must be *decoded by the receiver* in terms of his own experience (FRAMES 62-64, 135-148).

6   Language is a *frame of reference*: it can *mould our thoughts* by its limitations (FRAMES 76, 191).

7   Writing permits a subsequent *critical scrutiny* of written wisdom. Thought becomes more *objective*; it can be *stored* and *propagated over space and time* (FRAMES 79-81).

8 Printing enables the activities in 7 above to be done with *greater speed* and in greater numbers of *multiple copies* (FRAMES 101-102).

9 The '*Electronic revolution*', by means of radio, film, television and other facilities has put us back into a *world-wide non-literate communication system*—a 'global village'—according to McLuhan (FRAMES 104-108).

10 We can communicate wordlessly by means of the following devices—*art forms; action languages; eye contact; gestures; facial expressions; body appearance; posture; use of space; timing; touch* (FRAMES 112-127).

11 Information is a *flow of letters, sounds and statements* that helps to *reduce uncertainty in the recipient* (FRAMES 157-160). Entropy is a process of *disorganization or disintegration*—we try to bring about a state of *negative entropy* (FRAMES 161-163). Redundancy is *superfluous or repetitive matter* in communication (FRAMES 164-165). Noise is anything that *interferes with or reduces the fidelity of communication*; it may be *physical* or *semantic* (FRAME 166).

12 Information is a *flow* or *process*; knowledge is a *structure, the organized content of a memory* filled with selected information (FRAMES 151-153). Belief is a body of 'knowledge' which has *no information content* (FRAME 172).

13 Informatics is concerned with the *sociological and psychological aspects of information transfer,* especially in science and technology (FRAMES 167-170).

14 Rules of communication lay down *how communication shall be carried on* in a particular community; *with whom; when; with what content, nuances* and *expectations* (FRAME 186).

15 Communication cannot exist until there has been a *response* or *feedback from the recipient* (FRAMES 190, 194-195).

16 It would be desirable to *define a desired mental set*; to consider the *needs and interests of the audience*; to choose *appropriate concepts, language, examples, overall structure of argument, vocal variety, delivery, body language*; to abide by the *rules of communication*; to *eliminate noise* and to *promote helpful redundancy and feedback* (FRAME 209).

17 Mass communicators have the problems of: having *insufficient knowledge of their audience*; working within *large organizations*; having *no feedback*; *not knowing what the audience will choose to take from the transmitted material* (FRAMES 211-214).

18 Normal needs are: to *belong to a group*; to have a *degree of freedom*; to have *security, new experiences, success* and *appreciation*; to have *stable values*; to *participate in communication processes* (FRAMES 224, 232).

19 It forms an effective and ready-made *communication chain*; *rôle expectations* are not usually flouted; active communication offers a means of *analysing the work-load of the organization* (FRAMES 236, 258, 260).

20 Rôle expectations offer a *suitable context* for a message and assist in *its reception* and *decoding* (FRAMES 258-259).

21 *Decentralized circle*   *The wheel*

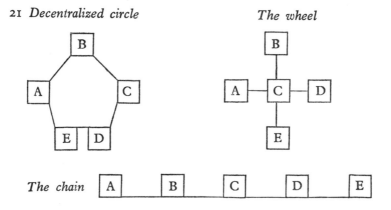

The chain

(FRAMES 262-264)

22 It must proceed *quickly*, through *open channels*; it must be *appropriate, clear, well-timed, correctly distributed* to all those concerned, *adequate* but *not too long* and *consistent with other related messages* (FRAMES 271-273).

23 A indoctrinates B in respect of 'p' (a debatable or controversial belief) *if B is made to believe 'p' without understanding the reasons for 'p'*. He may subsequently be *unable to believe 'not-p'*. These results may be brought about by *specially selected responses* (FRAMES 274-275, 305-308).

24 Barriers include *distance; climate; terrain; personal physical handicap;* differences of *language* and *social class; mental illness or deficiency* (FRAMES 276-287).

25 *Two persons* adopting *rôles* which may be considered to be *excessively interdependent* in a closed situation (FRAMES 334-335).

You might now be interested to compare your post-test score with your record of your pre-test score. All else being equal, this should give you some quantitative idea of your gain in knowledge as a result of reading through the program.

There now follow indexes to concepts, persons and titles which figure in the program.

WE HOPE THAT YOU HAVE ENJOYED THE TIME SPENT WITH OUR PROGRAM AND THAT YOU HAVE BEEN SATISFIED WITH THE RESULTS!

NOTES ON FURTHER READING

The literature on communication is voluminous so we offer a list which is a purely personal choice and does not require a specialist background.

Communication and communications (FRAMES *1-17*)
One of the most readable introductions to the problems of the communication process is David Berlo's *Process of communication* (Holt Rinehart, 1960) which gives among other things a very clear account of the problems of using communication models. For the important post-war influence of cybernetics on communication theory Norbert Wiener, *The human use of human beings* (Sphere books, 1958) is essential and interesting reading. In general, works on the psychology of communication tend to be hard going for the non-psychologist: exceptions to this generalization are John Parry, *Psychology of communication* (University of London Press, 1967) and a delightful collection of essays by George Miller, *The psychology of communication* (Penguin books, 1966). Wilbur Schramm, in the *Science of human communication* (Basic Books, 1963) collects together essays by such specialists as Leon Festinger, Elihu Katz, and Paul Lazarsfeld to give a lucid and comprehensive introduction to the problems of human communication. Floyd W Matson and Ashley Montague in *The human dialogue* (Free Press, 1967) present an overview of the general subject representing a wide range of disciplines including psychology, sociology, linguistics, cybernetics and information theory. The existentialist approach to communication is reflected in Lee Thayer, *Communication concepts and perspectives* (Macmillan, 1967) and also in Roslansky, *Communication* (North Holland Publishing Co, 1957). Other helpful and readable overviews are F X Dance, *Human communication theory* (Holt Rinehart, 1967) and K K Sereno and others, *Foundations of communication theory* (Harper, 1970). John Scupham's *Revolution in communications* is a personal analysis of the impact of communications on society, a theme which is treated further in Brenda Maddox, *Beyond Babel: new directions in communications* (Deutsch, 1972) which gives an entertaining look into the future when telephone numbers will be assigned to people, not places, when television sets will print out newspapers and cable television will bring widely scattered individuals together with a common purpose. Such transformations may mean the end of cities as dense information centres the communications problems of which are discussed by Richard Meier, *A communications theory of urban growth* (MIT Press, 1966). A work which we feel every student librarian

should read is Colin Cherry's *World communication: threat or promise* (Wiley, 1970). It is written in a popular style and gives helpful insights into the library as a facet of the social communication process.

Perception and communication (FRAMES *18-38*)
This is a very difficult area, with many works like D C Broadbent, *Perception and communication* (Pergamon Press, 1967). For the psychological background M D Vernon, *Perception* (Penguin books, 1962) is a useful introduction. There is an excellent introductory chapter on perception and attitude formation in David Krech and Richard Crutchfield, *The individual and society* which is reproduced in Wilbur Schramm, *Process and effects of mass communication* (University of Illinois, 1970). A standard work in this area is A R Cohen, *Attitude change and social influence* (Yale University Press, 1965) which could be usefully supplemented by Carl Hovland, *Personality and persuasibility* (Yale University Press, 1959).

Language, signs and symbols (FRAMES *52-127*)
By far the best introduction to this area is Stuart Chase, *The tyranny of words* (Methuen, 1938) and his later work, *Danger-men talking* (Parents Magazine Press, 1970). This could be followed by Roger Brown, *Words and things* (Free Press, 1969). Walter Nash, *Our experience of language* (Batsford, 1971) is a very readable work concerned with language as a form of social experience written especially for those readers who might be daunted by the technicalities of modern linguistics. To the student who is interested in a lucid account of the contributions of modern psycholinguistic theory there is an edited series of lectures given by such authorities as Colin Cherry, John Lyons and Basil Bernstein edited by Noel Minnis as *Linguistics at large* (Gollancz, 1970). Language is a prime concern of librarians and information officers and many articles reflecting this concern will be found by pursuing *Library literature* and *Library and information science abstracts*. There is now a rapidly growing literature on non-verbal communication, including a well illustrated and comprehensive work by Jurgen Ruesch and Weldon Kees entitled *Non verbal communication: notes on the visual perception of human relations* (University of California Press, 1969). There are also the classic works by E T Hall, *Silent language* (Doubleday, 1969) and *The hidden dimension* (Doubleday, 1966). For an introduction to symbolism and communication we recommend Susanne Langer's *Philosophy in a new key: the study of the symbolism of reason, rite and art* (Harvard University Press, 1967).

Communication: the involvement of the librarian (FRAMES *128-34*)
Until very recent times there has been very little interest in communication in librarianship theory. This is readily apparent in scanning such indexing tools as *Library literature* although, of course, there may be other relevant material embedded in related headings. Consequently most of the material is in periodical form. In pursuing the relevance of communication theory in librarianship (and we hope you will), a useful start might be made with Patrick Penland, *Communication for librarians* (University of Pittsburgh Library School, 1971); this might be followed by such articles as: Robert S Taylor, ' Question negotiation and information seeking in libraries' *College and research libraries*, May 1968: 178-94; Ellis Mount, ' Communication barriers and the reference question' *Special libraries*, October 1966: 575-8; E F Carter, ' Communications in a complex world' *Special libraries*, October 1961: 455-63 and Walter Carlson, ' Communication technology and libraries of the future' *PLA bulletin*, January 1969: 5-14. For an introduction to the function of interpersonal networks in the diffusion of knowledge and innovation there is a comprehensive overview in C E Nelson and D K Pollock, *Communication among scientists and engineers* (Heath, 1970) which could be usefully read in conjunction with D J de S Price, *Little science, big science* (Columbia University Press, 1963).

Meaning and information (FRAMES *135-70*)
As we have indicated in the text, information theory is a very abstruse area of study but the student may usefully read John Cohen and Ian Christensen, *Information and choice* (Oliver & Boyd, 1970) which brings together in a coherent framework such fundamental concepts as information, probability, decision, risk and search. J M Brittain, *Information and its users* (Bath University Press, 1969) is essential reading in this area and for an assessment of the function of information in social change there is the work by E M Rogers, *The diffusion of innovation* (Free Press of Glencoe, 1962). Articles on informatics are beginning to appear with greater frequency in periodicals such as the *Journal of documentation* and *Aslib proceedings*, and there is also a lucid summary by B C Brookes in *Five years work in librarianship* 1965-70. Robert Terwilliger's *Meaning and mind* (Oxford University Press, 1968) is a helpful introduction to the study of language and meaning; so also is J Wilson, *Thinking about meaning* (Heineman, 1972). A rewarding but difficult work is D M McKay's *Information and meaning* (MIT Press, 1969) and for those who wish to pursue the term ' meaning ' in the wider sense there is John

Hospers, *Meaning and truth in the arts* (University of North Carolina Press, 1946).

Communication, knowledge and belief (FRAMES *171-179*)
One of the main themes in contemporary Western culture, the breakdown of communication between man and man, is considered to be a by-product of the problem of knowledge: the problem, how do we know what we know? A start may be made in this area by using K J McGarry and T W Burrell's *Semantics and logic in the organisation of knowledge* (Bingley, 1972) and following this up by reading J P McKinney, *The structure of modern thought* (Chatto & Windus, 1971). Other useful readings would be E B Montgomery, *Foundations of access to knowledge* (Syracuse University Press, 1957); F Znaniecki, *The social role of the man of knowledge* (Harper, 1968) and D Peers, *What is knowledge?* (Allen & Unwin, 1972).

Communication, society and culture (FRAMES *180-191*)
There is a very readable collection of essays in Alfred G Smith's *Communication and culture* (Holt, Rinehart and Winston, 1966). There is a special viewpoint that social behaviour consists of reaction to symbols put forward in H D Duncan's *Communication and the social order* (Oxford University Press, 1962). Urban communications systems are discussed by Richard L Meier, in *A communications theory of urban growth* (MIT Press, 1962) and an historical survey is provided by Harold Innis, *The bias of communication* (University of Toronto Press, 1952). These works will serve as a useful preliminary to a more intensive reading of Jesse Shera's *Sociological foundations of librarianship* (Asia Publishing House, 1970) and *Libraries and the organization of knowledge* (Crosby Lockwood, 1965).

Inter-personal communication (FRAMES *192-200*)
The literature is rather sparse in this area but Michael Argyle's *Psychology of interpersonal behaviour* (Penguin Books, 1967) will repay study. Patrick Penland, *Communication for librarians* (University of Pittsburgh, 1971) treats the problem from the librarian's viewpoint and provides a helpful bibliography for further reading. The reference interview provides a classic instance of the problems of inter-personal communication in librarianship and information work and essential reading is Robert S Taylor, *Question-negotiation and information seeking in libraries*. Report no 3 (Lehigh University: Center for Information Studies, 1967). As a

follow up we recommend M J Brittain's *Information and its users* (Bath University Press, 1970).

Individual and group: mass communication (FRAMES 201-220)
Martin Carter's *Introduction to mass communications* (Macmillan, 1971) is a useful start and can be supplemented by the essays in K J McGarry, *Mass communications: selected readings for librarians* (Bingley, 1972). There is a wide inter-disciplinary approach provided by David Chaney, *Process of mass communication* (Macmillan, 1972), and Denis McQuail, *Towards a sociology of mass communications* (Macmillan, 1970) is a standard work in this field. For the importance of interpersonal communication in science, D J de S Price, *Little science, big science* (Columbia University Press, 1962) is essential reading.

Group motivation and cohesion (FRAMES 221-232)
There is a wealth of material in this area which embraces such problems as management communications and human relations. As a start we recommend L T Thayer, *Communication and communication systems* (Irwin, 1967) and then a survey of the field in Henry Voos, *Organizational communication, a bibliography* (Rutgers University Press, 1967) which gives annotated readings on decision-making persuasion, and network analysis.

Communication in hierarchies (FRAMES 223-275)
This section both overlaps and follows on from the previous one. As an introduction to the study of hierarchies we recommend Arthur Koestler, *The ghost in the machine* (Heinemann, 1967) and, of course, most texts on management deal with this topic among others. There was also a series of lectures *'Are hierarchies really necessary?'* printed in the *Listener* through July and August 1972. We also recommend Ludwig von Bertalanffy's *General system theory* (Penguin Press, 1968) together with D J Foskett's essay on the relevance of von Bertalanffy's theories to librarianship in *Journal of librarianship*: 4(3): July 1972 and his contribution on integrative levels in *The Sayers memorial volume* (Library Association, 1961) edited by D J Foskett and B I Palmer.

Barriers to communication (FRAMES 276-336)
For a depth study of the subject of this section, we recommend Jurgen Ruesch, *Disturbed communication* (Norton, 1957).

CONCEPT INDEX

References are to FRAME numbers.

INDEX OF PERSONS AND TITLES

For other names in the history of communication see the CHRONOLOGY OF COMMUNICATIONS immediately following the text.